HOW TO PREDICT
WHAT
PEOPLE WILL BUY

The Neighbors By George Clark

3-7

"It's a survey man asking what programs we watch.
What are some real highbrow programs?"

—*Chicago Tribune.*

HOW TO PREDICT WHAT PEOPLE WILL BUY

BY

LOUIS CHESKIN

DIRECTOR—COLOR RESEARCH INSTITUTE

With an introduction by
Van Allen Bradley

LIVERIGHT
PUBLISHING CORPORATION
NEW YORK

BOOKS by LOUIS CHESKIN

Color for Profit
Color Guide for Marketing Media
Colors: What They Can Do for You
How to Predict What People Will Buy
How to Color-Tune Your Home
Cheskin Color Wheel
Cheskin Color Charts
Living With Art

Library of Congress Catalog Card Number: 57-10751

PRINTED IN THE UNITED STATES OF AMERICA

To Bonnie Lynn

CONTENTS

7

CONTENTS

The Color Research Institute tests would have never come into being without the wealth of information about human behavior given to us by Psychoanalysis and Gestalt psychology.

There are now nine more years of experience in testing marketing media on an unconscious level. What has been learned in the last nine years? Have any new indirect testing techniques been developed? Are designers guided by the findings of unconscious level tests? Why do marketing men rely on unconscious level tests? Have the results of the tests that were conducted on an unconscious level in the past twelve years been confirmed by marketing experience? The purpose of this article is to answer the above questions.

In accordance with Color Research Institute recommendations, Mr. Akers first of all undertook the task of developing a Wilkins brand-identifying image, a symbol that would personify the high quality of Wilkins products.

Marketing tests have shown that changing the colors of a package to those with high prefer-

CONTENTS

ences and strong memory-retention (without changing the design) has resulted in great increases in sales.

Robert Stone, Vice President, National Research Bureau, Interviews Louis Cheskin

National Research Bureau Bulletin—January, 1956

Motivation Research is the type of research that seeks to learn what motivates individuals in making choices. It employs techniques designed to reach the unconscious or subconscious mind because preference generally is determined by factors of which the individual is not conscious.

Food Business—June, 1955

After we learn that the design as a whole is "optically effective" we proceed to determine its "psychological effectiveness." That is, we determine the consumers' attitudes to the design, which encompass a diversity of unconscious or subconscious, as well as conscious associations.

Industrial Packaging—November, 1955

Large corporations have been built with the aid of effective symbolism of imagery and color. Colors (and images) with favorable symbolism promote a product, a brand, a company. Wrong

CONTENTS

CONTENTS

He (Cheskin) pointed out clearly that sensation transference plays a major role in marketing. Unconsciously and consciously consumers are affected by color, abstract imagery, and realistic appeal imagery. This effect is transferred to the product or the brand. In other words, some colors and images suggest "strong," some suggest "weak." Some colors and images tell the subconscious or unconscious mind "good," some say "bad." Some colors and images tell the unaware consumer "mediocre." Some tell him or her "high quality," "delicious" or "healthful."

Besides his approach to color marketing, Cheskin takes a hearty whack at both the depth interview technique and esoteric designers.

"Remember that there is a difference between a consumer's stated opinion and her actual, unconscious preference," Mr. Cheskin warned, noting that preference involves self-interest, in making a choice, while opinion does not. Pref-

CONTENTS

erence means that the consumer actually wants the article, while her opinion does not necessarily mean that she wants it. Also, one stating an opinion often expresses what he or she believes the listener wants to hear. Thus, the institute does not interview, because too much depends on the skill of the interviewer, and does not poll, because people's opinions are not the same as their actual preferences. Further, verbalisms which people express are not the same as their actual behavior patterns.

CONTENTS

> Yellow, according to the findings of the insti-
> tute, has the highest "retention value" of all
> colors. That means that it hits you harder in the
> eye and you will remember it longer. But it
> doesn't make the customer buy because it has a
> low preference rating.

> All visual sensations produced by inanimate ob-
> jects are both sensations of imagery and sensa-
> tions of color. We want to learn, therefore,
> which type of images produce favorable sensa-
> tions and which unfavorable, and which types
> of colors produce favorable sensations and which
> unfavorable ones.

by Louis Cheskin and L. B. Ward, Director of
Admissions, Harvard Business School

Harvard Business Review—September, 1948

> In any case, there is today fairly general agree-
> ment among social scientists that many of our
> day-by-day actions are determined by factors of
> which we are not consciously aware. It is, of
> course, obvious to all of us that we forget most
> of the details of our daily experiences. What is

CONTENTS

not so obvious and is often overlooked is that
sometimes "forgotten" experiences leave traces
which continue to exert tremendous power over
behavior. In spite of the common acceptance of
the importance of psychological factors, many
current attempts to apply the methods of social
science to the problems of business and industry
still fail to take into account the unconscious
habits, purposes, needs, and motives that determine behavior.

INTRODUCTION

ASIDE from my longtime privilege of friendship with Louis Cheskin, one of the rewards of editing this exciting book has been the growing conviction, as I read and re-read its chapters, of its importance both as a manual of modern merchandising and as a significant contribution to contemporary business history.

As the title suggests, HOW TO PREDICT WHAT PEOPLE WILL BUY is first of all a most practical handbook in the use of tested techniques in marketing, advertising and selling. Just as importantly, it is an illuminating chronicle of certain revolutionary developments that have taken place in the last dozen years in the field of marketing research.

It has been my privilege to watch many of these developments at first hand. It has been my privilege also to write about Cheskin's role in these achievements, as well as to read extensively what others have written about him. The articles that I have selected as the chapters herein were written over the last ten years by and about Louis Cheskin and the Color Research Institute, which he heads. They have been edited to avoid a direct duplication of materials. Collectively they tell for the first time the step-by-step story of how

15

he developed his unique scientific approach to the use of design and color in selling merchandise.

Because this book sets forth an astonishing amount of useful information—actual findings of Color Research Institute on many specific elements of design and color as well as numerous case histories of success in moving merchandise—it should prove to be invaluable to every business executive, advertising man, sales manager, commercial artist or designer fortunate enough to discover it. At the same time, no collection of books on modern business, advertising or selling can henceforth be up-to-date without a copy. For these reasons, it should enjoy a widespread readership.

Louis Cheskin is no mere entrepreneur in the widely discussed field of motivation research as applied to marketing. A distinguished authority on color and art, he is also a trained psychologist and a trail-blazing social scientist. His employment of and perfection of laboratory and field techniques of psychoanalytic testing in the fascinating field of motivation research dates back almost a quarter of a century. His pioneering work in the field was carried out in the psychological tests with visual media which he conducted experimentally in directing a vast visual arts project under the auspices of the Chicago Board of Education.

The modern phase of his research activities dates from 1945, when he established Color Research Institute and began the direct application in the field of business of the techniques he had developed. As in all new research fields, there were periods of trial and error, temporary setbacks, fresh beginnings. But not for long. The quick growth to maturity of his "unconscious level testing" was signalized in September, 1948, with the publication of a seminal article on marketing research in the Harvard Business Review.

That article, "Indirect Approach to Market Reactions," was written by Cheskin in collaboration with L. B. Ward of the Harvard Business School. It reported the first three years' results in Color Research Institute's testing of individual reactions to colors and visual patterns in merchandising.

The significance of the Cheskin-Ward report was quickly apparent in marketing and advertising circles. For one thing, in this article and those that followed Cheskin gave to the fields of marketing research and market planning a new vocabulary grounded in psychology and psychoanalysis.

In none of the marketing literature before 1947 could be found such terms as "involuntary reactions," "unconscious mind," "unconscious level testing," "indirect approach," "motivation research," "sensation transference," "symbolism," "prestige identification," "ego involvement" and "ocular measurements." Neither have I been able to find any marketing literature that appeared before 1947 in which "the corporate image" or "brand identifying imagery" was given emphasis, or was even mentioned.

Those who are conversant with marketing and advertising are aware that within the last six years there has been a groundswell of interest in and recognition of the value of motivation research. Two of Cheskin's contemporaries who have done outstanding work in the field in the last half dozen years are Ernest Dichter of the Institute of Motivational Research in New York and Burleigh Gardner of Social Research in Chicago. Their contributions have helped to minimize the importance of large samplings of consumers as practiced by less scientific "pollsters." They have replaced head counting with a type of research now widely known as depth psychology.

Cheskin places considerably less emphasis on depth psychology than do these contemporaries, although he has joined with them in exposing the numerous fallacies of "opinion statistics" as dished up by the pollsters.

Instead of head counting or depth psychology, he has utilized a comprehensive system of carefully controlled tests, conducted on an unconscious level. Like depth interviewing, these tests are derived from Psychoanalysis and Gestalt, or image, psychology.

The articles selected for reproduction here trace the remarkable success he has enjoyed. These achievements have made history in the marketing and advertising fields. Many of the world's biggest manufacturers in their respective spheres have utilized his unique services to bolster sales of established products and to introduce new ones.

Some of the articles report the reseach on well-known marketing successes. One interesting case, not reported here but of which I have personal knowledge, is that of a breakfast food in which the findings of Color Research Institute were disregarded and Cheskin's recommendations were not followed. Tests conducted by the institute showed clearly that a proposed new package design for the item was inferior in marketing effectiveness to the old package. However, the company had employed two other research organizations, both of which came up with favorable reports on the new package design. The management followed their recommendations instead of Cheskin's. The result was that in less than one year the new package had to be withdrawn from the market and the old one reinstated.

In arranging the records of the successes for publication, I have reversed their chronological sequence. Thus the book opens with articles published in 1957 and representing twelve years of successful market testing. These articles do not explain theory. They reveal facts. They take up actual cases. In all the articles published after 1950, well-known brands of merchandise are discussed. In some cases, the research procedure is outlined.

It would be difficult to say which of the chapters in the book is most valuable for any one purpose. By necessity, some of the material presented discusses cases as well as principles that are covered in other chapters in somewhat different form. This circumstance arises because of the diversity of sources from which the material is drawn.

For the historian of social science as related to marketing research, the most significant chapters will be the two that discuss the origins of testing consumer attitudes, not opinions, and how consumers behave, not what they say. The two are "Twelve Years of Unconscious Level Testing," Advanced Management, May, 1957, and "Indirect Approach to Market Reactions," from Harvard Business Review in September, 1948.

In simple, straightforward language, Cheskin has set forth here the basic principles of psychological testing to insure business success. He has provided for business men a clear picture of the potentials in determining the marketing effectiveness of packaging, advertising and other selling aids. It seems certain that this new book will be standard equipment for the sales-minded executive for many years to come.

September 1957

Van Allen Bradley

Van Allen Bradley, noted literary editor and editorial writer for the Chicago Daily News, is the author of the business biography, "Music for the Millions: The Kimball Piano and Organ Story," published by the Henry Regnery Company of Chicago. He is director of the Institute of Business History.

HOW TO PREDICT
WHAT
PEOPLE WILL BUY

FOUR PILLARS OF SUCCESSFUL MARKETING

Advertiser's Digest—August, 1957

CHAPTER 1

THERE has been much said and written in recent years about marketing research by "marketing research specialists," more accurately, by those employed in the work of conducting "marketing research."

In their dissertations most marketing research people put emphasis on samplings of consumers and on statistics. The greatest part of "marketing research" consists of testing ads. Some test ad readership, others test ad appeal. For some reason, not worth exploring, the same researchers generally do not test both readership and appeal.

Readership is usually tested by means of a recall test or playback. Appeal is most frequently determined by interviewing samplings of consumers and asking them which of a number of ads has greatest appeal to them.

The playbacks are conducted on the assumption that, if an ad has a high readership score, it is an effective piece of advertising. Interviews on ad appeal are con-

Cheskin

MARKETING TREE

© 1957 COLOR RESEARCH INSTITUTE

ducted on the premise that the ad declared to be most appealing by the greatest number of the individuals interviewed is the most effective one.

Many marketing executives doubt that an ad with a high readership score necessarily means that it is an effective ad. Their doubts are based on at least one experience with a product that did not sell despite promotion with high readership score ads.

Other marketing executives are equally skeptical about "ad appeal interviews." They too have had failures after spending time and money testing to make sure that the ads to be used were declared to be most appealing by a large percentage of a carefully selected sampling of potential consumers.

"Research is not reliable," say those who have had unfavorable experience with research. "Research is a must in planning a marketing program," claim those who have had favorable experience with research. To the up-to-date and astute marketing executive the question is not whether to have research. His question is, what kind of research?

Those who blame research for marketing failures are guilty of fallacious thinking in two respects. One, that advertising is the only factor in the success or failure of a marketing program and, two, that every activity called research is reliable research.

It is natural, and at the same time unrealistic, for an advertising man to claim that effective advertising is the only factor in a successful marketing program.

It is also natural and equally unrealistic for a package

designer to assume, as some do, that an effective package is all that is needed for success in marketing a consumer product.

It is as natural and as unrealistic for a manufacturer to believe that the consumers will rush to buy his product because it is of superior quality.

And the marketing manager is being unrealistic also, if he proceeds on the assumption that lowering the price necessarily means an increase in the volume of sales.

A marketing program cannot stand on one or even two pillars. It must have four pillars and four walls, each buttressed with reliable research.

The pillars of successful marketing, listed in order of importance, are:

1—Product Quality.
2—Package Appeal.
3—Promotion Effectiveness.
4—Price based on psychological, sociological and economic factors, as well as on cost.

A product, of a quality as good as or better than that of the competition, is the first requisite of a successful marketing program. Pouring millions of dollars into promoting an inferior product will not bring continuous consumer acceptance. A widespread and effective advertising campaign of an inferior product may get some to buy the product the first time. Repeat sales depend primarily on product quality.

However, actual product quality is one thing; impression of product quality is another. A product of the very best quality will not be a marketing success if the package does not express the quality. The package is the visual manifestation of the product. The package characterizes the product to the consumer. Vision is the strongest of the senses and the visual impression the product or brand makes on the consumer is a vital factor in consumer acceptance.

Effective advertising plays its full role only in promoting a high quality product in a package that is an effective marketing tool. Effective advertising dramatizes the package. It builds package identity. It associates the package with favorable symbolism. It incorporates copy to arouse interest and to instill desire. None of these things can be accomplished in an ad without a package that expresses high quality and that has imagery (and also color for some products) of specific identity and great appeal.

If we analyze some basic aspects of semantics we can easily see that pricing is a psychological, sociological and economic problem as well as a cost factor. For example, when a woman says that an article is cheap, she means that it is either low in price or of inferior quality, or both. Usually she means it is both low in quality and in price. Individuals often use the words costly and precious synonymously. Expensive and high quality are frequently used as synonyms.

Prestige identification should be given consideration in pricing. High price often goes with high prestige as well as with high quality. The social and economic conditions of the country are important factors in prestige identification, a particularly important element in marketing gift items. Twenty years ago an object costing $2 was generally considered an appropriate birthday or graduation gift. Under present socio-economic conditions a $5 article is generally considered more appropriate.

The following are examples of pricing related to prestige identification:

Two books of similar character, appealing to a special type of book buyer, were published. One was a great success, the other a failure. Yet the book that had a wide sale sold for $5 and the one that had failed sold for $2. The publishing cost was the same for each of the two books.

There were a number of minor factors involved in the distribution of the two books. However, the major factor was that the $5 book was generally bought as a gift. The $2 book was not bought as a gift because individuals interested in buying or receiving this type of book would not look upon a $2 investment as sufficiently worthy of being considered a gift.

Another vital factor in the sale of the two books was the fact that the bookseller made a $2 profit on the $5 book. He made only 80¢ on the $2 book. He, therefore, displayed the $5 book and promoted its sale.

How does one know he has a high quality product? How does one find out whether his package is an effective marketing tool? How does one make sure that the advertising will be potent? How does one decide what 'the retail price should be? The answer to all these questions is research, reliable research.

There is no reason for taking up space here to discuss the need for product research. Many of those who started business without research facilities or without having the services of independent product research laboratories are out of business.

Package research is, however, another matter. The package became a major marketing factor only in recent years, with the rise of self-service markets. The package is now a vital marketing factor because it is a selling tool. It is the silent salesman; often it is the major sales medium.

Many marketing people still are not fully aware of the importance of the package as a marketing tool. Although most marketing managers give lip service to the importance of the package, many still look upon the package as a mere container.

Another reason that the package does not yet generally receive scientific treatment or is not objectively measured as a marketing tool is that it is associated with creative art or design. Many still consider art and science as separate and unrelated entities. The concept still is prevalent that true art and creative expression are not to be put to objective or scientific tests. The traditional concept is that art has its own reasons for being. It is not subject to the rules and principles of science. Because of temperament, early conditioning and education, artists generally object to putting their creations to scientifically controlled testing.

Still another reason why a majority of the packages in the supermarket are not effective marketing tools is that packages put through marketing research were not tested by reliable, controlled and psychologically sound methods.

What is commonly still called marketing research consists of interviewing housewives, asking them which of a number of packages they like best. Such marketing research is often worse than no research at all, because it gives one a false sense of security. Scientifically controlled tests have demonstrated that individuals cannot tell what influences them. Shoppers are not aware that they are influenced by a color or an image. They are not conscious of the effect a package has on them.

Sensation transference is a common occurrence in the supermarket. The shopper transfers the sensation from the package to the product. She is not at all aware of doing that. She does not know that the imagery, color and design caused her to take that particular package.

In interviews, people try to give logical reasons and rational or sensible answers. In the supermarket emotional factors are there playing their parts. Unconscious or subconscious motivations take over.

By testing with psychoanalytic techniques on an unconscious level, we learned that consumers are influenced favorably or unfavorably by images such as triangles, ovals, circles, crests and crowns. Often a slight change in the image changed the psychological effect from favorable to unfavorable or vice versa.

Tests conducted on an unconscious level revealed

that colors produce favorable and/or unfavorable reactions. Changing the dominant color on a package may increase the consumer's acceptance of the package by from 50 per cent to 500 per cent. We have many examples of such increases in consumer acceptance.

Conducting tests on an unconscious level means that the individuals are not aware that a test is being conducted or they do not know what is being tested. The tests are designed so that the individuals react naturally and spontaneously, without inhibition and minus elements of ego involvement and prestige identification.

A change in the package design will mean a great increase in sales, only if the change is made on the basis of tests, conducted on an unconscious level, showing that the new package is optically effective and psychologically more favorable than the old one, and also, if all other marketing factors remain about the same.

One of the important other marketing factors is the nature and character of the advertising. The only way of knowing whether an ad will be effective is by testing it with potential consumers. Testing does not mean, however, asking opinions. It means conducting the test on an unconscious level. It means testing not only readership or recall, but testing consumer attitudes. It means finding out the kind of favorable or unfavorable associations consumers have with the ad. Actually, the test should (and would) determine consumer reactions to the brand or product as presented by the ad.

Reliable ad testing is unconscious level testing which shows whether the ad is effective in introducing the product or brand to the consumer. A test conducted on an unconscious level shows clearly whether the ad makes the consumer want to try the product.

I believe I should remind the reader that at the time of testing the ad there should be no question about the effectiveness of the package. The package should always be a significant part of the ad and the effectiveness of the ad depends greatly on the effectiveness of the package or label.

Research can also be used to determine price. As I pointed out before, consumers associate price with quality. I used to be amazed to note how consumers associated a high price with one design or object and a low price with another design or object. Yet the cost of producing one design was no greater than the other. Such associations no longer surprise me.

In a competitive situation it is often necessary to have a low, unprofitable price. However, it is advisable to base the price on consumer attitudes that are revealed in a test conducted on an unconscious level and not on the basis of cost or competitive factors. The test may show that your package upgrades your brand. It may reveal that you can get more for your product than your competitor because your package suggests much higher quality.

Under present-day marketing conditions there should be no question about using marketing research. The only question is: What kind of research?

Research conducted on the assumption that people can tell how they are affected by an image, a color or a design should not be honored with the name research. Modern psychology and psychoanalytic findings in particular have demonstrated that people are motivated unconsciously. The real motivations are hidden deep in the subconscious. People cannot tell us about their attitudes. Individuals generally cannot put their feelings into words. Consumers cannot tell us how they are influenced by a design or affected by a color.

Research can tell us whether consumers really like the product (which is not the same as merely saying they like it), whether the package will be an effective marketing tool, whether the advertising is potent and whether the price for the article is right, neither too low nor too high. The tests, however, must be conducted on an unconscious level.

ORIGINS OF UNCONSCIOUS
LEVEL TESTING

Advertising Agency Magazine—July, 1957

CHAPTER 2

LIKE many students of psychology in the late twenties, I was fascinated by Watson, Kohler and Freud. The diverse principles of these three giants in the realm of psychology confused me for some time and frustrated my feeble attempts to formulate a psychological yardstick for measuring and evaluating human behavior.

As I delved deeper into psychology, I became more and more aware of the vastness of the field and the meagerness of actual knowledge specialists had of human behavior.

Sigmund Freud is the father of Psychoanalysis. But, a number of psychoanalytic principles were contributed by Freud's contemporaries, Alfred Adler and Carl Jung. Later Sullivan, Fromm and Horney modified a few of Freud's original theories. Although these pioneers of Psychoanalysis disagreed in many respects they all put emphasis on the unconscious or subconscious mind as the motivating force.

ORIGINS OF UNCONSCIOUS LEVEL TESTING

One of the tools developed by the psychoanalysts for probing into the unconscious mind is the association-type test. Nearly all psychoanalysts use association tests as a means of discovering attitudes, uncovering unconscious urges and determining the behavior pattern of an individual.

The association-type test is one of the psychoanalyst's favorite tools because it reveals much about the person being tested. Doctors have found it to be one of the most reliable diagnostic devices.

In 1935 I began conducting experiments with various association test forms for determining reactions to creative art and design. In 1945 the association-type test was adopted by Color Research Institute for testing marketing media—packages, ads, posters, etc.

Max Wertheimer, Wolfgang Kohler and Kurt Koffka were the leaders of a school of psychology known as Gestalt (image). This school of psychology, like Psychoanalysis, deals with the complexities of human behavior. However, its basic principle is simple. It stresses the interdependence of component elements and demonstrates the importance of grouping.

Most of us have been inculcated in our early years with the belief that the whole equals the sum of its parts. This is still taught in most of our schools as an indisputable fact. Gestalt psychology has shown that the whole is different from and more or less than the sum of its parts. It demonstrated that the effect of the whole depends not only on its parts but also on their arrangement.

This Gestalt (image) principle is a major factor in the Color Research Institute's testing procedures. The Gestalt principle is the reason why we test separately the basic image, every color and the reading matter to ascertain the degree of effectiveness of each and, after we find that each component element is as effective as it can possibly be, we begin testing various arrangements of these elements.

We generally find that different arrangements of the same elements produce different effects. Often we find that some of the arrangements produce favorable effects and some make unfavorable impressions.

Although the basic principle and procedures of Color Research Institute tests are derived from Gestalt psychology, the testing techniques are borrowed from Psychoanalysis. The primary tests for determining consumer attitudes are association tests designed and conducted so that the consumers in the sampling react spontaneously. For solving some marketing problems indirect preference tests are used, which are so designed that the consumers in the sampling are not aware of what is being tested.

The indirect preference test is conducted completely on an unconscious level. In some indirect preference tests the participants think we are testing a product whereas actually we are testing the package. The consumers transfer the sensation from the package to the product in the container without being aware of doing so. Acceptance or rejection of a product or brand is often caused by the package. If the label suggests that the food in the can is of high quality, the consumers find that the taste is to their liking. If the label on the can is associated with low quality, they find that the contents are of inferior grade. Color Research Institute preference tests have demonstrated this hundreds of times.

In addition to the sensation transference type of preference tests, Color Research Institute conducts indirect preference tests that are designed so that the consumer makes a choice without knowing that the choice is of interest to anyone but himself.

The concept of probing into the unconscious, the principle of sensation transference, the association test technique and all indirect procedures of testing originated in Psychoanalysis. The concept of the true meaning of the whole in relation to its parts and the realization of the full significance of organization or arrangement in perception have been demonstrated by Gestalt psychology.

I stated at the beginning that I was also absorbed in the theories of Watson. In the twenties John B. Watson, the founder of Behaviorism, was the most controversial figure in the world of psychology. According to Watson, heredity is of minor or no importance. A child is born with nothing except the capacity to absorb impressions and to develop habits and patterns of behavior instilled in him by the adults with whom he comes in contact.

After Watson made a name for himself in the realm of psychology and in educational circles, he entered the field of advertising.

Until recent years the Watson school of psychology dominated almost the entire advertising profession. According to the Behaviorism theory of Watson, the consumer had no inherent attitudes towards anything. Therefore, the advertiser could build attitudes and develop habits in the consumer.

Constant repetition is considered by Watson's followers as the basic principle for all advertising. According to this theory the habit of buying a particular brand can be inculcated in consumers by constant repetition of an ad or slogan. According to this theory, the adult consumer has no preconceived ideas, has no inherent capacity to make any decisions, either objective or subjective, and he behaves almost completely in accordance with advertising-conditioned reflexes.

Psychologists have long discarded Watson's theories and modern educators no longer take Watson seriously. However, many advertising men still conduct advertising campaigns according to Watson's theories. Many do not even dream they are practicing Behaviorism, but their advertising strategy shows the Watson influence quite clearly.

We know now that an individual's behavior is conditioned by heredity, early upbringing, including kind and degree of parental love and affection, education and economic status. Psychoanalysis has demonstrated that individuals have strong likes and dislikes and often deep-seated fetishes and phobias. Some have an abnormal attachment to a particular color or image. Others have an abnormally strong dislike for a certain color or shape. Most consumers do not have extreme aversions (phobias) nor abnormal attachments to objects (fetishes). However, people differ in their preferences. They react differently to the same object. Some objects have wide appeal, other articles, images or colors appeal only to a few.

Psychoanalysis and experience have taught us that some attitudes in individuals generally cannot be changed. Prejudices cannot easily be eliminated and new ideas are easily accepted only if they are not in conflict with deep-seated habits or concepts.

The following are three out of many examples demonstrating that consumer attitudes are not always conditioned by an advertising campaign.

In 1935, when I first began testing color preference, magenta red had a preference rating of above 90. Chartreuse rated 12. During the war, when many dyes were difficult to obtain, manufacturers spent fortunes in advertising chartreuse, normally accepted by only 12 per cent of the populace. After millions of dollars were spent in promoting chartreuse, marketing tests showed acceptance of chartreuse by only 18 per cent. Magenta red still rates above 90 in preference. Most reds had more than 80 per cent acceptance 100 years ago and 20 years ago—and they have the same wide appeal and high acceptance today.

Many image tests are conducted at Color Research

Institute. One series of tests showed that a triangle brought out unfavorable associations in women. When the corners of the triangle were rounded, however, the associations were mostly favorable. The tests proved that most women react favorably to a triangle with rounded corners and unfavorably to a triangle with sharp points. The kind of triangle design on a package obviously has an effect on the consumer without advertising entering the picture.

The diverse attitudes toward the two triangles are unconscious. Consciously the busy housewife does not care whether the triangle has sharp points or rounded ones. She will tell you, if asked, that she does not concern herself with such nonsense. If you probe further, she will let you know that she does not even care about the package. She is not interested in the design or the color. She is interested only in the quality of the contents, the product. What is more, she believes what she tells you. She is actually not conscious of the fact that she is influenced by the package, that she transfers the sensation from the package or the imagery or the color to the product.

Consumers were shown two packages that differed only in one respect, one having an illustration of the product on the front panel, the other a crest. Both packages were in all other respects alike. They were asked this (psychologically unsound) question: Which one do you like better and why? A great majority said they liked the package with the product illustration because they could see what was in the package.

ORIGINS OF UNCONSCIOUS LEVEL TESTING

In Color Research Institute association tests conducted on an unconscious level, the results were exactly the opposite. The package with the crest was associated with high quality and the package with the product illustration was associated with an inferior product. Obviously, the crest denoted high quality without the benefit of advertising.

Psychological tests and experience have shown that consumers do make some rational choices. To some degree consumers can differentiate between an inferior and a superior product. Consumers normally can at least smell some products. They know when an object gives long service or deteriorates in a short time.

But more often, however, choices are made unconsciously. Sensation transference plays a great role in the market place and in the home. Advertising gives prestige to a brand, which is an important factor in marketing. But it is equally true that most of the purchases are made on impulse. In the store, the consumer is motivated by drives other than prestige identification.

Advertising men (and women) who are still under the spell of Watson, and many of them are, knowingly or unknowingly, "test the ads" before publication, according to the Behaviorist theory. They usually conduct "playbacks" with a sampling of potential consumers on the premise that if an ad is recalled by a large per cent of the consumer sampling, the ad will motivate a large number of individuals to become actual consumers of the advertised product or brand. To followers of Watson, familiarity equals acceptance. In many advertising agencies marketing research still consists of conducting recall tests or playbacks. (Other agencies prefer opinion polling.)

One should not assume that Behaviorist psychological concepts still exist only in the advertising field. Our educational systems are still permeated with Watson influences. Although the practice of memorizing (without understanding or believing) goes back to ancient times, Watson gave this practice respectability. He endowed it with "scientific" terminology and bestowed upon it the stamp of modernism. Memorizing and imitating are stressed in most of our schools, not thinking, creating or evolving ideas.

Even now there are many university graduates who have been indoctrinated with Behaviorist concepts, although most may not be aware of the fact that Watson conditioned their thought channels.

About 12 years ago, when Color Research Institute first advocated the use of the principles of Gestalt psychology and the techniques of Psychoanalysis in marketing research, the Behaviorist-oriented specialists resisted with all the strength at their command. Some still resist. Since 1945, however, many advertising specialists and researchers have come to accept the contributions made by Gestalt psychology and Psychoanalysis.

Progressive marketing men and alert advertising men acknowledge the full meaning of imagery (Gestalt). They now realize that consumers think of a company or brand in terms of a company or brand image. They recognize now that people do not get to know the corporation; they only become familiar with the corporation symbol. Consumers identify a brand by the image associated with the brand, whether the image is a simple one or a complex one consisting of a variety of elements.

Gestalt psychology points out that the total image makes the impression. The total image, or Gestalt, depends on the grouping or arrangement as well as on the component elements themselves. Gestalt psychologists have found that people are often conscious of images. In other words, company images or brand identifying images often have an effect on the conscious mind. Individuals are frequently aware of the effect an image, or Gestalt, has on them.

Gestalt psychology has demonstrated that there are rational aspects in human behavior.

Color Research Institute tests show that consumers are nearly always conscious of appetite appeal illustrations and of beautiful young women. Both men and women are generally aware that they enjoy looking at and are influenced by an illustration of luscious roast beef or by a beautiful figure.

Psychoanalysis also puts emphasis on the importance of imagery. Psychoanalytic studies have shown clearly that people "think" in terms of images. They act in accordance with image impressions. They react to images, not to ideas. That is, an individual reacts to the image of an idea, actual image, or his imaginary image of the idea. The image, real or imaginary, is a symbol with favorable or unfavorable connotations.

We now know, thanks to Psychoanalysis, that we are

not always conscious of the symbols that affect our behavior. Most of us are rarely aware that our attitudes are influenced by and our preferences are prompted by symbols. Rarely is one aware that he is influenced by a color, an abstract shape or a crest.

Gestalt psychology has found that people are affected by images consciously and Psychoanalysis has shown that individuals are affected by images unconsciously. Gestalt psychologists put emphasis on the arrangement or grouping of component elements into one image impression. Psychoanalysis puts emphasis on the emotional significance of images as symbols.

Tests conducted at Color Research Institute and by others have demonstrated that the reactions of human beings are neither all conscious and rational nor all unconscious and irrational. However, we have ample evidence that, statistically speaking, human reactions are to a much greater extent unconscious than conscious. Individuals usually react unconsciously.

There are now a number of market researchers who reject the Behaviorist theories and are conducting tests according to Gestalt and psychoanalytic principles. Within my knowledge, however, they all use depth interviewing techniques, not basic unconscious level tests.

Psychoanalysis deals with depth psychology. However, depth psychology is a tool for probing into the emotional stability of an individual. It is a technique for delving into a person's past, as far back as his early childhood. It is a diagnostic device for testing sanity or for measuring the degree of normalcy in a person.

ORIGINS OF UNCONSCIOUS LEVEL TESTING

At Color Research Institute we are not occupied with mental health. We are not seeking to psychoanalyze individuals so that we can aid them in becoming more rational human beings. We are not attempting to help people solve their emotional problems.

We are merely seeking to find out how consumers react to a company or brand image. We are concerned with learning consumer attitudes toward a package, an ad, a color or a trademark.

There are many weaknesses in depth interviewing, even if the great cost is disregarded. Depth interviewing gives the respondents time to build up defense mechanisms, in which the ego and prestige identification factors play important roles. Depth interviews are often influenced or biased by the interviewers. A depth interview is not equal to a buying situation. Shoppers do not have discussions in the store. They are affected visually. They merely react. They are motivated by images which they could not possibly discuss because they are not conscious of the effect these images have upon them.

Still another weakness in some motivation research is that it deals with the total image and not at all with the component elements individually. It rarely pinpoints a specific weakness, because the respondents are exposed to and react to the total package or ad.

Also, within my knowledge, none of the depth interviewing specialists have developed means for testing involuntary reactions. They assume that potential consumers will be attracted by a package, poster or ad because they react favorably when it is in front of them.

Tests have shown that this concept is just as untrue as the point of view of the Watson-influenced researchers, who assume that people will react favorably to a brand or product and will accept it if it gets attention and is easily recalled.

More than twenty years ago, we found that the association-type test, the sensation transference test and other types of indirect preference tests are reliable techniques for determining consumer attitudes. We found that optical instruments are the most practical and reliable means for measuring the involuntary reactions of consumers. We have been using optical instruments for twelve years for measuring the involuntary reactions to a package or ad before putting it into a field test to determine its psychological effect.

Involuntary reactions do not involve associations. Involuntary reactions are merely sensations; they are not perceptions. The degree of visibility a package has from the shelf and the extent of readability, that is, the ease or difficulty in reading the brand name, are inherent in the character of the package. The flow of the design or the eye-movement is inherent in the package.

The color and contrast determine the degree of visibility. The kind and size of letters, the spacing plus the color contrast, determine the readability. The arrangement or positioning of the elements determines the eye-movement. Thus, the measurements of visibility, readability and eye-movement are involuntary on the part of the person participating in the test.

ORIGINS OF UNCONSCIOUS LEVEL TESTING

Color Research Institute tests have demonstrated that:

1. In order to isolate weak elements from strong ones, we must test the component elements separately.
2. In order to ascertain the effectiveness of the whole (package or ad) we must test the whole.
3. Before we are ready to determine consumer attitudes to a package or ad, we must be sure that the involuntary reactions to it are favorable.
4. Unconscious level tests are the only means for determining consumer attitudes.

The Color Research Institute tests would have never come into being without the wealth of information about human behavior given to us by Psychoanalysis and Gestalt psychology.

TESTING PACKAGE EFFECTIVENESS

PRESENT PACKAGE – COMPETITIVE PACKAGE – NEW DESIGN

COMPONENT ELEMENTS

INVOLUNTARY REACTIONS

READABILITY

PSYCHOLOGICAL EFFECT

{ IMAGE PREFERENCE
IMAGE RETENTION
IMAGE ASSOCIATION

{ COLOR PREFERENCE
COLOR RETENTION
COLOR ASSOCIATION

{ BRAND NAME IDENTITY
BRAND NAME ASSOCIATION
BRAND NAME RETENTION

PACKAGE OR DESIGN AS A WHOLE

INVOLUNTARY REACTIONS

VISIBILITY

EYE-MOVEMENT

PSYCHOLOGICAL EFFECT

{ QUALITY ASSOCIATIONS
PRICE ASSOCIATIONS
ACTUAL PREFERENCE

OCULAR MEASUREMENTS

OPTICAL INSTRUMENTS

FIELD TESTS

ASSOCIATION   INDIRECT PREFERENCE
RETENTION   SENSATION TRANSFERENCE

TWELVE YEARS OF UNCONSCIOUS LEVEL TESTING OF PACKAGES AND OTHER MARKETING TOOLS

Advanced Management—May 1957

CHAPTER 3

The First Three Years of Unconscious Level Testing

IN THE article, "Indirect Approach to Market Reactions," published in the September, 1948, issue of Harvard Business Review, L. B. Ward, director of admissions of the Harvard Business School, and I discussed unconscious factors of behavior (in the supermarket or self-service store).

The inadequacy of the direct approach to determine how people will react to an object—package or ad—was covered in that article. Factors determining purchases were outlined. Abstract factors influencing behavior in special (marketing) situations were pointed out. Meanings and motivations were analyzed in the light of testing with indirect techniques on an unconscious level.

In 1948 Color Research Institute, the source of most of the information in that article, had had three years of experience in testing actual marketing media on an unconscious level. Before 1945, the indirect methods were used in testing colors and images as such, unrelated to specific brands and independent of the limiting elements of established logotypes and mandatory selling copy, which are integral parts of every package or ad.

There are now nine more years of experience in testing marketing media on an unconscious level. What has been learned in the last nine years? Have any new indirect testing techniques been developed? Are designers guided by the findings of unconscious level tests? Why do marketing men rely on unconscious level tests? Have the results of the tests that were conducted on an unconscious level in the past twelve years been confirmed by marketing experience?

The purpose of this article is to answer the above questions.

What Has Been Learned in the Last Nine Years?

One of the important conclusions that was drawn from tests conducted after 1948 is the necessity for determining the involuntary reactions to a package or ad before taking steps to ascertain consumer attitudes towards the marketing tool.

Marketing specialists have always been aware of the importance of impact. They know that for a package or an ad to be effective, it has to be striking, it has to attract attention and sustain a degree of interest. However, reliable tools for measuring these attributes of a marketing tool were lacking until recent years.

After many devices, methods and techniques had been tried, optical instruments were found to be most reliable for determining involuntary reactions to a package or other marketing tools. Optical instruments are now used to measure three aspects of a package—visibility of the package as a whole from the shelf, readability of the brand and product names and eye-movement which shows how the design guides the eyes and where it holds and does not hold attention.

Another recent development is the use of accumulated data on color and imagery. Much information has been gathered about specific colors and images which serves as a basis for initial evaluation of a specific color or image on a package. It is no longer necessary, for example, to conduct a test with consumers to find out whether an oval or a rectangle is a more effective framing device. Tests conducted in the last twenty years have consistently shown that of the two geometric images, the oval is the more effective device. It has greater preference and greater retention in the memory. Association tests have shown that ovals have predominantly favorable associations and rectangles have largely unfavorable associations.

Association ratings are important because they affect preference. For example, an orange-red without a specific association rates low and magenta red rates high. However, in the kitchen or in association with a kitchen product, orange-red has a higher preference rating than magenta red.

There is now available much data on geometric images, such as ovals, circles, triangles. Many tests have been conducted with many types of images and it has been found that modification of an image has a definite effect on consumer reactions.

However, because images have limitless possibilities for variation and modification there is not nearly as much information available on images as there is about colors with specific identity.

Because accumulated information on a color or an image can be applied to many problems for many products, color and image ratings are not costly.

Ocular measurements to determine involuntary reactions are made with little effort and are therefore also obtained at low cost. Because involuntary reactions do not involve associations and complex psychological factors, only a few individuals are needed for the ocular tests. However, more than one individual must be used in the ocular tests because there is no assurance that any one person chosen has normal vision. It has been found that it is necessary to use three to six individuals for measuring involuntary reactions to a package.

It is now possible to make some judgments just on the basis of ocular measurements, plus color and image ratings. An analysis at this point may show the need for new designs, complete or only slight revision, or it may indicate further testing.

UNCONSCIOUS LEVEL TESTING

If the ratings of the component elements of a package are favorable, that is, if it is found that the colors and brand identifying image rate high and if the package rates excellent or good in visibility, readability, and the eye-movement test, it is then necessary to learn the psychological effect of the package as a whole because the whole is different from and more or less than the sum of its parts.

It is and always has been evident to some in the packaging field that it is essential to determine the effectiveness of components of a package, that it is necessary to learn which specific element is strong and should be retained and which is weak and should be eliminated or replaced with a strong element. However, it had been traditionally assumed that the whole is the sum of its parts and therefore it was taken for granted that the package as a whole was good or effective if each component part of the package was found to be good or effective.

Gestalt psychology has demonstrated that the whole is different from and more or less than the sum of its parts. This Gestalt psychology principle is now being applied in marketing research. The recent application of this principle in testing packages and ads is one of the most important contributions to marketing research. It is one of the major reasons for the reliability of present day market testing.

Another vital addition to the arsenal of marketing research is the association-type test, which was born in the field of Psychoanalysis and has been modified and developed in recent years to serve as an aid in market testing. The association-type test has been found to be the most effective device for discovering consumer attitudes and for obtaining unconscious reactions.

To meet market testing needs, pioneers of association-type tests have developed controls that make it possible to conduct the tests on an unconscious level. Each test consists of two parts. One part is a control. It is planned to be of interest to the individuals in the sampling. It is a device for winning the interest of the consumers. It is presented so that those in the sampling react spontaneously to the control part of the test and to the actual object (package, ad or trademark) being tested. There are additional controls incorporated into the design of the test. The association test is conducted so that the participants react naturally, without inhibition and defense mechanisms entering into the test situation. They merely check a number of attitude words, favorable and unfavorable, in association with the package, design, image, color, trademark, etc.

Experience has shown that it is advisable for the control part of the test to have little or no copy. The objective is to make sure that the participants in the test are not aware of the commercial purpose of the test or that the test is being conducted for a client. In this respect, Color Research Institute has a clear advantage because its name in no way suggests marketing research.

After a little experience with association-type tests it became evident that it was necessary to have a special test design with specific attitude words applicable to each type of product. That is, special association test questionnaires have to be designed for food products, toiletries, soaps, etc.

The consumer samplings are divided into a number of classifications—socio-economic, age, sex and geographic area. The statistics are usually broken down in accordance with the consumer sampling classifications. An association test report, specifically one from Color Research Institute, contains some pages showing the total favorable and total unfavorable attitudes. There also are pages listing attitude words according to rank, that is, those showing the greatest number of reactions or specific associations at the top and those having the smallest number at the bottom.

Although an association test report is statistically comprehensive and shows many aspects or sides of consumer reactions, experience in dealing with management has shown that the analysis has to be concise. The statistical part of a Color Research Institute report, which covers a sampling of from 800 to 1,200 consumers in at least four parts of the country, consists of from 30 to 120 pages. The analysis generally consists of one page. The report is presented so that the client can make his own analysis if he wishes to do so.

Occasionally it is found that an association test is not conclusive. To meet such a situation an indirect preference test has been developed. The indirect preference test is designed so that the consumers participating in the test think one thing is being tested whereas actually it is something else. For example, a test is conducted on colors for a living room. The participants become involved in an interior decoration test, which is so designed that the participants incidentally reveal their reactions and attitudes to the objects being tested. Often the participants are asked to choose a prize from a number of objects. Their choice, which is made in the realm of self-interest, is what is really being tested.

Most indirect preference tests are designed to ascertain sensation transference from the package to the product. The test is planned so that the impression given is that the product is being tested, whereas actually the containers or packages are. The consumers unconsciously transfer the sensations from the package to the contents.

For example, in a test of three coffee packages, 86 per cent of the women wanted one of three coffees because they felt it was the best. Actually, all three coffees were the same—only the containers differed.

Another example of sensation transference is a test in which 97 per cent of a group of women claimed that a pat of white butter "tasted oily like margarine" and a pat of yellow margarine "tasted like butter." This is an example of transference of a visual sensation to a taste sensation.

Sensation transference from the package to the contents is a common occurrence in the supermarket. That is why indirect preference tests are designed to reveal the difference in kind and degree of sensation transference (from the package to the product) of a number of packages.

UNCONSCIOUS LEVEL TESTING

Ocular measurements for determining involuntary reactions are now almost universally recognized as essential aids in developing an effective package. The accumulated information on colors and images is widely used. Association-type tests are now well known and indirect preference tests or sensation transference tests are now recognized as a reliable means for ascertaining actual consumer preference. All these marketing research tools have reached maturity in the last few years.

Pioneers in unconscious level testing made progress as rapidly as they did because they borrowed freely from the fields of Gestalt psychology and Psychoanalysis. Their experiments consisted mainly of adapting Gestalt psychology principles and psychoanalytic techniques to the field of marketing research.

Unconscious Level Testing and Depth Interviewing

Since "Indirect Approach to Market Reactions" was published in September, 1948, there has been much printed and said about motivation research or, as some say, motivational research. Most of the exponents of motivation research employ depth interviewing techniques. The basic difference between depth interviewing and the traditional interviewing or polling is that in the former the emphasis is on qualitative factors, whereas in the latter the emphasis is on quantitative factors.

Many research men, among them the author of this article, find that depth interviewing is not a technique that is reliable or practical. Experiments showed that when a person knew he was being interviewed he rationalized and set up all sorts of defense mechanisms in which ego elements and prestige factors played decisive parts. It was also found that the depth interviews were biased by the interviewers.

There were indications that the degree of error in depth interviewing depended to a considerable extent on the limitations of the particular interviewer. Astute marketing analysts often drew conclusions from depth interviews quite successfully. However, in the opinion of many, a marketing research technique is not a practical technique when it is dependent on the special skill of an individual.

Testing since 1935 has demonstrated conclusively that people are motivated by all sorts of factors of which they are not aware and since they are not conscious of these factors they cannot tell about them. In most instances, people cannot say whether they like or do not like something, because they are not aware of its effect on them. In other words, consumers cannot tell that they are moved to buy a product by a color, an image or a design, because they don't know that they are motivated by it. Few consumers are aware that they transfer the sensation from the package to the product.

The following case is an excellent illustration of the inability of people to tell what they prefer and it also shows that verbal indifference is very misleading.

Each woman in a group who participated in an interior decorating contest was offered a purse as a prize.

The purses were available in four colors—red, green, blue and yellow. "Which color do you want?" each woman was asked. Of the group of forty-nine women, fourteen said they wanted red, eleven said blue, five yellow and two green. Seventeen of the women said, "I don't care which color I get."

The women were later asked to come up to the counter to choose their purses. The fourteen who said they wanted red, took red. The eleven who said they wanted blue, took blue. Of the five who said they wanted yellow, one took red, one took blue and three took yellow. Of the two who said that they wanted green, only one took green and the other red. Of the seventeen who said they didn't care about the color, twelve took red purses and five took blue ones.

In a direct interview type of research those women who expressed indifference would likely not have been counted. Actually, these same consumers revealed that the red purses had the highest preference, the blue ones the second highest. The green and yellow purses actually rated lower than they would have if those who expressed indifference to the colors had been omitted from the total.

Over twenty years of testing experience has shown that people reveal their preferences and attitudes in spontaneous expressions and in unconscious reactions. In situations in which there are ego-involvements, in which prestige identification factors are present and in which defense mechanisms play a part, we should not expect expressions of real preferences or true attitudes.

An individual may be of the opinion that a hamburger and onion luncheon is "tasty" and a lobster Newburg luncheon is "unappetizing." But when asked which she or he considers to be a better luncheon, hamburger and onion or lobster Newburg, the answer may be the latter, because it has higher social standing, it has prestige identification. Whenever socio-economic factors get into the testing picture, we are confronted with prestige identification factors.

It was found that generally individuals do not like to admit ignorance. When a housewife is being interviewed she strives to appear intelligent. She does this because her ego is involved. That is, her ego prompts her to want to appear intelligent.

The following is an excellent example in which ego-involvement and prestige identification played important roles.

Before yellow margarine was available on the market, five thousand women were asked whether they would use margarine if it were colored yellow. Over 90 per cent said they would not.

There is little doubt that a large number of the housewives were aware that they did not know what they would do if yellow margarine were actually available. However, because of ego-involvement, they did not say, "I don't know." Each wanted to give the impression that she knew what she wanted, although she was aware that she did not know. Many of the respondents thought that they would use yellow margarine, but most of them believed they would lower their social positions in the eyes of the interviewer by saying they would like to have a less expensive spread than butter.

There is much evidence that frequently a person uses words to conceal true feelings. Sometimes he tries consciously and deliberately to hide an attitude. Often the individual is not aware of trying to conceal his feelings.

For example, smokers were interviewed about two package designs for cork tipped filter cigarettes. One package carried a crest on the front panel and the other package an illustration of a cork tipped cigarette. In all other aspects the packages were alike. The smokers were asked, "Which of the two packages do you prefer for this brand of cigarettes and why?" Most of the respondents expressed a preference for the package with the illustration because, most of them said, they could see what was in the package. However, in association tests, conducted on an unconscious level, the package with the crest rated much higher than the one with the cigarette illustration. Few could or would say that a crest influenced their choice but the association test showed that, unconsciously, the crest determined their choice.

Over twenty years of testing experience has shown conclusively that a consumer sampling of 100,000 or over will not produce reliable results if the 100,000 or more individuals are asked to judge designs or colors, because these individuals then are not reacting naturally to the designs or colors. They become critics, each

61

of whom wants to give the impression that he is logical and practical and has good taste.

Actually, in the buying situation, the consumer generally acts emotionally and compulsively, unconsciously reacting to the ensemble of colors, images and designs, which in the subconscious are associated with the product.

Because consumers transfer the sensations from the package to the product or brand unconsciously, they cannot tell anything about the relationship between the package and the product. Tests must, therefore, be conducted on an unconscious level.

It was found that depth interviews did not eliminate the ego-involvement and prestige identification factors. Furthermore, because more time was given in the depth interview than in an ordinary interview, there was more opportunity for the individual to build up his "defense mechanisms."

There is much evidence on the unreliability of depth interviewing. One example: An organization using depth interviewing techniques and an organization using unconscious level testing techniques were employed to make a study of the marketing effectiveness of a trademark in the form of a little girl and of an advertising campaign featuring the little girl with certain movie stars. The depth interviews and the association tests showed almost identical results on the movie stars. On the little girl, however, the depth interviewers arrived at conclusions exactly the opposite from the association test results. The depth interviewers found that consumers did not believe the little girl was real. They recommended not using her as a trademark. However, the association tests, conducted on an unconscious level, showed that she had the greatest number of favorable associations and fewer than 2 per cent unfavorable associations. The little girl has since become a very effective trademark.

Testing experience in recent years has led to the conclusion that testing should not be only quantitative, with emphasis on samplings of thousands of consumers, or only qualitative, limited in size of sampling to fewer than several hundred consumers. Each marketing test must be both qualitative and quantitative at the same time.

Reactions to visual media follow socio-economic, cultural, educational, sex and age patterns but it has been found that samplings of many thousands of consumers are not needed. Experience has shown, however, that in testing a national brand consumer samples much smaller than one thousand are generally too small.

An association test with a carefully chosen sampling reveals specific favorable and unfavorable associations consumers in general will have with the marketing tool. It reveals a wide gamut of consumer attitudes. The association test is usually conclusive.

The indirect preference type of test has always proved to be effective in cases where the association test did not bring out conclusive results.

Some indirect preference tests are "visual impression" tests, some are "product in use" tests. The test with the three coffee containers, mentioned at the beginning of this article, is an example of a product in use test. The interior decorating contest, in which purses were offered as prizes, is an example of a visual impression test. Both types of tests reveal important aspects of consumer behavior. The visual impression test is equal to the store or buying situation. The product in use test shows whether the visual impression or the sensation transference (from package to product) is lasting.

The indirect preference test gives a white or black answer. It shows that a majority of consumers want the package or that they don't want it, but it does not pinpoint reasons for consumer rejection or acceptance. It does not reveal specific consumer attitudes. In this respect, it has the same limitations as point-of-sale testing. However, an indirect preference test costs much less than going into a test market and it is much more reliable than a point-of-sale test conducted in three or four stores. Also of vital importance is that an indirect preference test does not reveal marketing plans to competition. Point-of-sale testing does.

Testing experience during the last twelve years has shown that a combination of association tests and indirect preference tests is a most reliable means for determining consumer reactions to a package. The indirect preference test is completely on an unconscious level. The sensation transference from the package to the product is wholly unconscious. The association test, however, reveals a range of consumer attitudes which is illuminating and of great aid in drawing conclusions.

Are Designers Guided by Unconscious Level Research?

A designer's creativity and originality are his greatest assets. Paradoxically, these are also the designer's greatest faults because he often tries to advance too far into the future. Often, a redesigned package loses brand identity.

We have evidence that most people enjoy change, but they are shocked by drastic change. To be effective, a package design for a brand must be original. It must have distinct character and specific identity. At the same time, it must appeal to the great majority of people who are not interested in design as such yet they are unconsciously influenced by it.

A modern package is designed for display. Display is a visual medium for influencing people.

Because package designs are produced by individuals, artists and designers, who are by nature, education and conditioning subjective, objective marketing research must be used to determine the effect the design has on typical or average consumers.

However, most designers believe or claim that they know how consumers will react to their creations. Some assume that the objective is to create a design in good taste. One well-known designer declared that he was designing for tomorrow. Therefore, he said, there was no use in testing with consumers of today.

Experience in working with designers has shown that most of them consider research with consumers a necessary evil. Evil in that the research is used to check the value of their creations and necessary only because their clients want to have actual evidence that the proposed design will be an effective marketing tool.

Some designers with national reputations reveal great naïveté about the psychological factors in designs to be used for marketing. Many designers get opinions from their friends and their wives, assuming that this is research.

The following is taken from a letter written to a client by a director of a well-known package design studio.

"We had a poll on the two package designs with all the designers in our studio. They agreed unanimously that the round package is much better than the rectangular package."

Obviously, the socio-economic factors and education factors of consumers, the unconscious mind and indirect testing methods meant nothing to the writer of this letter.

Some designers are openly hostile to all research. Others talk about research and use it only when the client insists that it be used.

However, there are designers who want to avail themselves of all the objective information they can get to aid them in developing a package, trademark or product that will have maximum success in the market.

66

UNCONSCIOUS LEVEL TESTING

Why Marketing Men Rely on Unconscious Level Tests

Most merchandisers know that the package is no longer a mere container. They are aware that the present-day package is a sales tool. But what kind of package is an effective sales tool? What should the package look like in order to sell a particular product? That is a vital question in present-day marketing.

In the market place each stack of packages has a pattern of colors and images producing sensations that have a strong influence on the shopper, almost always on an unconscious level. Up-to-date marketing people know that rarely is a consumer aware that she is influenced by the color and design of a package.

The following are some of the reasons why many package designs are not effective marketing tools.

First, a designer is a highly trained individual with a much more highly developed sense of design than that of the typical consumer.

Second, designers have had considerable training in the graphic arts but have had little training in the optics and psychology of color and imagery.

A third reason is that until recent years there has been little scientific knowledge about the effects of colors. Only in the last twenty years has there been any serious attempt to study the optical and psychological aspects of color.

The fourth reason is that designers (also marketing men) "think" about packaging designs. The average or typical consumer merely reacts to them. The "expert" judges, the ordinary consumer feels. The specialist tries to be logical, the housewife is basically emotional.

The fifth and most important reason is that in order to determine the effect of a package (or an ad) on consumers, a complex, controlled procedure of testing with a carefully chosen sampling of consumers must be used.

Merchandisers no longer depend on marketing experts because they have found that many experts know or think they know how consumers reacted to an old package but they cannot predict how the majority of consumers will react to a new package which has a new ocular pattern and almost certainly a totally different optical and psychological effect.

Nearly all marketing men know that marketing research is needed in order to determine which of a number of package designs is an effective marketing tool and which is not, which ad will bring desired results and which will fall short of achieving the objective. But what kind of marketing research?

Surveys are conducted with the assumption that people know what affects them and on the premise that they can tell how they will react. We know now that individuals are generally not aware that they are affected by color and design and that they cannot tell what they will do.

Depth interviews are much too leisurely, too verbose and too intellectualized. They are removed from and are totally different from a real shopping situation. In the supermarket, shoppers act quickly and unconsciously, without verbalizing.

Unconscious level tests are designed to equal or approximate the shopping situation.

Association tests (derived from Psychoanalysis) have proved to be most effective devices for revealing consumer attitudes. They are effective because they do not give the individual an opportunity to bring out defense mechanisms. They bring forth the person's unconscious, uninhibited, unguarded reactions. Various devices are used as controls to keep the tests on an unconscious level.

Indirect preference type tests have been found to be a reliable technique for determining preference; in this kind of test the consumer makes the choice without knowing that the choice is significant in any way to anyone but himself. As I pointed out, most indirect preference tests are sensation transference tests, which are totally unconscious. That is, the consumers in the test sample are completely unaware that they are transferring the sensation from the package (or copy) to the contents or product.

Systematic, controlled, unconscious level testing has in the last twelve years demonstrated its effectiveness in predicting how consumers will react to a package, a trademark, a color or color combination, an ad and other visual marketing tools. Management uses unconscious level tests because it finds these tests a reliable means for discovering consumer attitudes and reactions. For twelve years marketing executives have used unconscious level research as a guide in making marketing decisions. The sales results have confirmed the reliability of the unconscious level testing techniques.

Marketing Experience Confirming Unconscious Level Test Results

Marketing success depends on a number of factors besides the package or trademark. In addition to distribution facilities and sales personnel, the major marketing factor is first of all the product itself or the quality of the product.

Next in importance is the package, because the package symbolizes the character of the product. It expresses the nature or personality of the product. In self-service markets the package is the silent salesman.

Third in importance is the kind and amount of advertising and promotion. These are third in importance because an extensive advertising program and potent promotion can be effective only if the product and the package fulfill the promise of the advertising and promotion literature. As stated before, the package represents the product. Through sensation transference the package becomes the product. The package is the visual manifestation of the product.

Still a fourth major factor in marketing is price. The price of an article is often based on psychological factors as well as on cost factors. Generally the price has to meet competitive prices. Research and experience have shown that in many cases it is advisable to upgrade a product with a package that symbolizes high quality and to sell it at a higher price. There are a number of products which showed increased sales after they had been given high quality packages and higher than competitive prices.

Because of the complexity of modern marketing, it is not always possible to attribute the success of a brand entirely to a new package, to a new trademark or to a new color.

However, the following are examples of brands that have had phenomenal successes after only one major change in the marketing picture. In some cases it was the package, in others the trademark or the color. Each of these marketing successes was predicted by Color Research Institute tests. Each of these successes was brought about by developing a package, evolving a trademark, or choosing a color, on the basis of association tests and indirect preference tests. When a package or trademark design was the problem, the entire battery of ocular measurements, color ratings and field tests was used for eliminating weak package designs and adopting the design that rated high, or rated higher than competitive packages or trademarks.

Example 1. Lux Toilet Soap in Pastel Colors.

Tests of the colors of the Lux toilet soap and the tests of wrapper designs showed that the Lux toilet soap in four colors would be a great success. The tests showed that the market was ripe for toilet soap in pastel colors derived from four hues that are optical and psychological primaries. The association tests showed that the Lux toilet soap pastel tints met the psychological needs and wants of the American consumer. The Lux toilet soap colors were adopted after extensive research. The specific tints were chosen on the basis of tests conducted on an unconscious level.

Example 2. White Lux Toilet Soap.

Ocular measurements and association tests showed that the new foil wrapper would be a very effective marketing tool. Its great success is now well-known to marketing people.

Example 3. Sunbeam Bread (Quality Bakers of America).

Tests conducted on an unconscious level showed that Miss Sunbeam is a very effective brand-identifying image and that the wrapper is a very effective marketing tool. Quality Bakers of America are doing exceptionally well.

Example 4. Marlboro Cigarettes.

Tests conducted on an unconscious level indicated that Marlboro cigarettes in the new package should have from 500 per cent to 1,000 per cent increase in sales. The increase was much greater than that.

The advertising agency's campaign was no doubt largely responsible for the additional increase. The agency used the research findings very effectively in planning its advertising program.

Example 5. Dove.

Association tests showed that Dove, a Lever Brothers product, would be a great success. The field tests showed that the package rated outstandingly high in association with high quality. It is now well-known that Dove is very successful.

Example 6. Blue Star Potato Chips (Blue Star Foods, Inc.).

The vice-president of the Blue Star Foods, Inc., states in a letter to Color Research Institute, "Our sales are ahead of last year on the new Blue Star bag line by about 15 per cent, but, as stated above, we have held back on promotions." This is an excellent example of the importance of the package in present-day marketing. The new bag that passed "ocular" and "field" tests increased sales in spite of the fact that promotion was reduced drastically.

Example 7. Betty Crocker Cake Mixes (General Mills, Inc.).

The following was published recently about cake mixes: "Tests and analysis (made by Color Research Institute) showed General Mills that Betty Crocker's brand identification was weak: It lacked the connotation of quality and there was little family identification. In 1954, the company retained an outside design firm —Lippincott & Margulies—who recommended the use of a 'spoon' symbol. Last year General Mills increased the quality connotation by the use of a larger and better product illustration without diluting brand identification or family identity. In the field of cake mixes alone the total market more than doubled in the last two years. The Betty Crocker cake mixes quadrupled in the same period. Each design change was researched by Color Research Institute of Chicago. In addition, the

73

major design changes were tested in a limited number of stores."

Example 8. Good Luck Margarine (Lever Brothers).

There were three major changes in the Good Luck margarine package. It was reported that each change brought, or was coincident with, from 100 per cent to 200 per cent increase in sales.

Example 9. Imperial Margarine (Lever Brothers).

This is an example of a high quality package that symbolizes a high quality product and is sold at a higher price. The package was developed by Lever Brothers with the aid of unconscious level tests. The high price did not keep it from becoming a very great marketing success.

Example 10. Bissell Carpet Sweepers.

This is an example of color being the primary factor in increasing sales. "Experts" predicted doom for non-electric sweepers. Association tests showed that treating non-electric but efficient sweepers with high preference colors would increase sales greatly. The recent success of the Bissell Company with its "color-tuned" sweepers is now widely known.

Example 11. Consoweld Corporation.

Consoweld surfacing laminates are an excellent example of scientific color use. The colors for the Consoweld surfacing materials for kitchen counters, bathroom walls, table tops, etc., were chosen on the basis of psychological tests (of the association-type) with consumers. Also, the patterns were tested with consumers on an unconscious level. By approaching their marketing problems through research conducted on an unconscious level, the Consoweld Corporation achieved objectives (that some people considered unattainable) of limiting the number of colors and patterns, thus keeping the inventory at a minimum and of more than doubling business in less than a year.

Example 12. Standard Oil of Indiana Trademark.

The trademark consisting of a torch and oval in red, white and blue passed all tests with very high ratings. To say that the company has used this trademark successfully is superfluous.

There are many more brands that have become great successes mainly because of the package, the color or the trademark that had been developed with the aid of systematic, controlled, unconscious level research. Some of the other companies that have used to advantage unconscious level research are: General Electric Company; The Warren Company; Universal Potteries; Felt & Tarrant Manufacturing Company; Club Aluminum Products Company; Hawley and Hoops; Scott Paper Company; Adams Pleasure Foods; Gerber Products Company; Mars Confections; General Foods Corporation; The Nestlé Company; D.W.G. Cigar Corporation; Orchard Industries; Ferry-Morse Seed Company; Pet Milk Company; Roman Meal Company; Borcherdt Malt Extract Company; California Walnut Growers Association and J.A. Folger & Company. There are still many other large and small companies, too numerous to mention, that have profited from unconscious level testing.

REDESIGN THROUGH TESTING

Coffee & Tea Industries and The Flavor Field—January 1957

CHAPTER 4

THE JOHN H. WILKINS CO., Washington, D. C., has been marketing high grade coffee and tea for many years. In conjunction with their advertising agency, M. Belmont Ver Standig, an examination of all packages was undertaken recently. On the recommendation of Mr. Ver Standig, the Color Research Institute of Chicago was selected for testing the effectiveness of the designs and colors.

John H. Wilkins, Jr., president, wanted objective information. The coffee cans, bags and jars and the tea cartons were sent to Color Research Institute headquarters in Chicago.

The institute's tests showed that the packages' brand identification and colors could be greatly improved.

Louis Cheskin, director of the Color Research Institute, wrote an analysis of the research and made specific recommendations for redesigning. He also presented a list of designers who could do the job of creating effective packages with the aid of the research.

REDESIGN THROUGH TESTING

The Wilkins management chose Charles Akers of Chicago to design new packages for the entire Wilkins line.

In accordance with Color Research Institute recommendations, Mr. Akers first of all undertook the task of developing a Wilkins brand-identifying image, a symbol that would personify the high quality of Wilkins products.

He produced a number of Wilkins image designs which were submitted to the Color Research Institute for testing. One image design came out with very high test ratings. It was a special kind of oval, a Wilkins oval. It was characterized by a smooth, appealing, attention getting "W" at the top.

The designer's second task was to develop a new Wilkins logo. The research showed that the old logo was heavy and angular and had negative associations.

Mr. Akers was striving to create an elegant, smooth, flowing logo that would reflect the high quality of the brand. The designer submitted a number of logo designs to the Color Research Institute, and these were put through ocular tests. One of the logo designs came out with exceptionally high ratings.

The third step was for the designer to develop complete designs for three coffee cans—one for each grind, for three coffee bags, for instant coffee jars and for tea cartons. For this third step in designing the packages Color Research Institute provided the designer with test-rated colors, colors that rated high in preference and in retention.

Finally, the completed designs were put through ocular measurements. Each of the package designs rated high in visibility, in brand name readability and in the eye-movement tests. This meant that consumers' involuntary reactions to the packages were good.

Then the packages were put into an unconscious level, association-type field test. This test revealed that consumers had favorable associations with the packages. The packages successfully expressed the high quality of the brand.

All Color Research Institute tests, the ocular measurements and the field tests were conducted on an unconscious level, a technique in which the institute pioneered. The tests are designed so that consumers react to the package as spontaneously and as naturally as they do in stores.

The new carton for tea bags has a convenient reclosing device. The carton is made of Foiline, aluminum foil laminated to boxboard by a special process, and is produced by the Gair Cartons Division, Piermont, N. Y., of the Robert Gair Co., Inc., manufacturer of paperboard and paper products.

The one-piece carton has glued end panels, one of which is uniquely perforated to form a reclosing device after the carton is opened. The top flap of this panel can be tucked into a die cut opening in the lower flap. The customer can use the carton as a receptacle in the home and be sure that the product is being kept fresh.

The shimmering silver foil becomes part of the smart blue, white and red printed design. The design features an oval logotype incorporating a "W" in its outline, and a tea bag showing the number of bags the carton contains.

The design is printed horizontally on one side and vertically on the other to make the carton adaptable to variously sized display shelves. Directions for making hot and iced tea are printed within the logotype on one end panel.

Wilkins coffee is now being packed in American Can Co. key-open vacuum containers with new, brightly lithographed color—complementary labels that permit the housewife to select her favorite grind at a glance. The cans also feature Canco's new easy-opening beaded tear strip.

The "new dress" features identifying colors for the three Wilkins grinds: orange for drip grind, blue for fine grind and brown for percolator grind.

The new Wilkins packages were evolved from a co-ordinated plan of operation. They are an excellent example of what can be accomplished by a combination of research-minded management, an alert advertising agency, progressive packaging manufacturers, a practical-minded designer and a scientifically controlled systematic research.

THE MEANING OF COLOR

Supermarket Merchandising—November 1956

CHAPTER 5

COLOR effect is on an unconscious level. People are not aware that they are affected by color or how they are affected by specific colors.

Experiments and tests with colors conducted in the last twenty years have shown that each specific color has a distinct psychological effect on people. A color has a direct effect on an individual's emotions.

Psychological tests show that blue, and tints, shades and tones derived from blue, produce an effect of coolness, distance and airiness. Some blues are sedative and others depressing. Red, and colors derived from red, produce a feeling of warmth, nearness and intimacy. Some reds are stimulating, others irritating.

Tests conducted under controlled conditions show that yellow has the greatest visibility and attention-getting power. Most yellows rate low in preference, but rate high in memory-retention, and some yellows cause eyestrain and fatigue. Certain tests reveal that colors have subconscious as well as conscious associations.

THE MEANING OF COLOR

Some colors are associated with high quality, some with low quality. Some produce pleasant associations and others produce unpleasant associations.

More than twenty years of color-testing has taught us that some hues increase in preference when they are diluted with white, some decrease in appeal. For example, when orange-red is mixed with white, the preference rating for the color is much higher than that of pure orange-red. When magenta red, which rates very high in preference, is mixed with white the result is a color of very low preference.

Some colors increase in appeal or preference when deepened with black, other colors decrease in preference. For example, add black to orange-red and you get a high preference brown. Add black to magenta red and you get a low preference purple. Add black to green and you get a deep green that often rates about the same in preference as the green without black.

Optical and psychological tests show that some color combinations are easy on the eyes and have greater appeal than the individual colors themselves. Other color combinations are hard on the eyes and have very low appeal.

Marketing tests have shown that changing the colors of a package to colors that rate high in preference and in memory-retention (without changing design) has resulted in great increases in sales.

After putting high preference colors on articles for the home, sales increased greatly.

If color is such a great factor when used in small

doses on small areas of packages and articles, it certainly is a factor on large areas—walls, counters and floors of a supermarket.

Some colors aid in displaying merchandise. Others camouflage and hinder the display. Some enhance the products. Others detract from their appeal. Some are easy on the eyes and psychologically satisfying. Others are hard on the eyes and are psychologically negative.

In short, color is like a magnet—it can attract or repel. Use the right colors and you'll encourage the shoppers to stay in your stores longer and buy more items. Use the wrong ones and you'll make them want to get out as quickly as they can.

QUESTIONS AND ANSWERS ABOUT MOTIVATION RESEARCH

Robert Stone, Vice-President, National Research Bureau
interviews
Louis Cheskin, Director, Color Research Institute
National Research Bulletin—January 1956

CHAPTER 6

Introduction

EVENTS of the past 12 months have proved that motivation research is here to stay.

As a relatively new marketing tool it has withstood the storms of controversy, not yet subsided.

Such renowned names in the field of market research as Alfred Politz and Dr. Ernest Dichter have debated the value of motivation research.

But there is still another name to be acknowledged, that of Louis Cheskin, director of Color Research Institute and a pioneer in motivation research. In the last ten years Louis Cheskin has played a major role in a number of well-known marketing successes.

The purpose of this interview is to help clarify moti-

THE FOUR PILLARS OF PROFIT

PACKAGE

The package is a silent salesman. To be an effective marketing tool it must be seen, it must be liked and it must be remembered.

PRICE

The price should be based on psychological as well as on cost factors.

PRODUCT

The quality of the product is first in importance for getting repeat sales – in building brand acceptance.

PROMOTION

Advertising means building brand identity and familiarity. To be effective, advertising, like the package, must be seen, must have appeal and must be easily recalled.

vation research, the techniques employed and the results achieved.

Q—There has been a great deal of discussion on motivation research. Would you give a definition of this type of research?

A—Motivation research is the type of research that seeks to learn what motivates individuals in making choices. It employs techniques designed to reach the unconscious or subconscious mind because preference generally is determined by factors of which the individual is not conscious.

Q—What do you think of what Alfred Politz had to say about motivation research?

A—Judging from the headline of an article I have read, Politz condemned motivation research. However, I believe, he was actually condemning a specific technique of motivation research, not motivation research itself. The value of this type of research depends greatly upon the technique employed.

Q—Do you agree with Mr. Politz that depth interviewing as advocated by Dr. Dichter is not a reliable technique?

A—Yes, I hold the same opinion as Mr. Politz on this matter. My conclusion that depth interviewing is not an effective technique is based on considerable experience with this technique. The great danger in depth interviewing is that the deeper you dig, the bigger the hole you make to fall into. The degree of error depends upon the limitations of the interviewer. However, in my opinion, Dr. Dichter is an astute marketing analyst, probably one of the best analysts we have. He can often draw conclusions quite successfully when he handles the problem personally. However, when a research technique is dependent primarily on the special skill of an individual it is not a practical technique. To put it more directly, depth interviewing is not reliable because when a person knows he is being interviewed he rationalizes and sets up all sorts of defense mechanisms, in which the ego, prestige and still other factors play their parts. The results from depth interviews are influenced by the particular and too often limited skills of the interviewers.

"Consumers Cannot Tell What Motivates Them"

Q—I have read your article in the Sept. 1948 issue of the Harvard Business Review and I have read about Color Research Institute testing methods in "Color Guide for Marketing Media," but I don't know how to describe the kind of motivation research used by Color Research Institute for determining the marketing effectiveness of packages and ads. What do you call your motivation research techniques?

A—Our methods are best described as unconscious level testing or indirect techniques. We use association-type tests, indirect preference tests and retention tests. All the tests are conducted on an unconscious level. People are motivated by all sorts of factors of which they are not aware and, since they are not conscious of these factors, they cannot tell you about them. People cannot say whether they like or do not like something when they are not aware of its effect on them. In other words, consumers cannot tell us that they are motivated by a color, an image or a design because they don't know that they are motivated by it. We, therefore, use testing methods that reveal consumers' feelings and attitudes about which they cannot talk. We employ indirect techniques, procedures in which the actual tests are on an unconscious level. For example, no one will ever say consciously that he buys a certain brand of cigarettes because of the crest on the package and few will say that they buy Marlboro cigarettes because they like the package. Yet, in our field tests conducted on an unconscious level of several different Marlboro designs, we discovered that the pack with the crest rated far higher than the package designs without crests. We test component parts of a package or ad, the brand identifying image, the brand name, before testing the package as a whole. We test the whole, the entire package or design, after we learn that each component part is in itself effective.

Q—Are the testing techniques used by Color Research Institute original methods of yours?

A—Not at all. Perhaps our techniques are original in the field of marketing research, but there is nothing original about them in the field of psychology. Testing the component parts first and then the whole is based on a Gestalt psychology principle that the whole is the sum of its parts plus. In other words, the whole is more or less than and different from the sum of its parts. We are pioneers in using association tests in market testing. However, association tests are not new. They have been used by psychiatrists and psychoanalysts for many years.

Q—Alfred Politz said that all consumer research must start with ideas or hunches. What is your opinion of this?

A—Designers, copywriters and company managers provide us with the ideas and hunches. As research people, we make no assumptions of any kind. Our job is to find out how consumers react to whatever is submitted to us for testing.

Q—Mr. Politz labeled motivation research a "pseudo-science." You don't agree with him on that, do you?

A—I still believe that Mr. Politz was talking about depth interviewing, not motivation research. In depth interviews, ten interviewers may be as different from each other as the 100 individuals they interview. However, in unconscious level testing, we employ controlled procedures to find out how a number of representative individuals react to a specific unit without their being aware that we are particularly interested in their attitudes toward that unit, package, design or ad.

"Marketing Research Should Be Both Qualitative and Quantitative."

Q—Mr. Politz charged that motivation research interviews are often made with small and unrepresentative samplings of the population. What about this?

A—This is not true in our case. Our minimum samplings are 600 persons for a national brand. For the various phases of Marlboro we interviewed, if our procedure can be called interviewing, about 5,000 cigarette smokers and in our tests of a number of Philip Morris designs we had samplings of about 6,000. I question whether we can consider our procedures interviews because the individuals who participated in the cigarette package design tests, for example, were not made aware that we had any particular interest in Marlboro or in Philip Morris.

Q—Then you think it is necessary to poll several thousand people before drawing conclusions?

A—Not at all. Generally, 600 is enough. It depends on the nature of the product and on the competitive factor. I must also point out that polling is not the word. We don't poll. Polls reveal to us what people say they will do, not actually what they will do. The two are not the same. Perhaps you recall that this point was brought out with many examples in the September, 1948, Harvard Business Review article. I also discuss this subject in my books, "Color Guide for Marketing Media" and "Color for Profit." However, surveys, "nose counting," direct question and answer type of research have an important place in marketing research. Motivation research is not needed when, for example, the purpose is to find out how the grocers in a specific area display a line of packages.

Q—Don't many research organizations use much larger samplings than 600 or even 6,000 individuals?

A—Yes, they do. We have data on colors and on some images based on tests with over 100,000 individuals. However, samplings of many thousands of consumers are generally not needed in unconscious level testing. And even a sampling of 100,000 will not produce reliable results if the 100,000 individuals are asked to judge designs, colors or ads, because these individuals then are no longer typical consumers but critics, each of whom is most likely to want to give the impression that she is logical, or practical, or that she has good taste. Actually, in the buying situation, the consumer generally acts emotionally and compulsively, unconsciously reacting to the colors, images and designs which in the subconscious are associated with the product. Because consumers transfer the sensations from the package to the product or brand unconsciously, they cannot tell us anything about the relationship between the package and the product and we must therefore conduct the tests on an unconscious level. Testing is not or should not be either only quantitative, with emphasis on samplings of thousands of consumers, or only qualitative, limited in the size of sampling to fewer than a hundred consumers. Each marketing test must be both qualitative and quantitative at the same time. Testing on an unconscious level with a sampling of several hundred consumers generally meets both qualitative and quantitative requirements.

Q—*How do you account for the fact that so many research people don't believe in motivation research?*

A—Those who don't believe in motivation research

are not familiar, or have not kept pace with the advances that have been made in the field of psychology. It merely shows a lack of knowledge of the progress that has been made in the realm of psychology. Specialists in psychology have learned much in the last thirty years. Psychologists have developed a number of techniques for measuring human reactions.

Q—Is every package submitted to you for research tested in the field with at least 600 consumers?

A—No. Most packages and designs submitted to us for testing never get into field tests. We don't recommend field testing for a package until it passes ocular measurements and until we have applied to it our accumulated information on its colors and imagery. A package goes into field testing only if it has the best possible visibility from the shelf, plus good brand name readability and if it passes an eye-movement test, and if the brand identifying image and the colors rate high in preference, retention and association.

"Component Parts of a Package Are Tested to Discover Specific Weaknesses and Strengths."

Q—Why is it necessary to test the imagery, color, visibility, and readability separately in addition to testing the package as a whole?

A—We test the component parts of the package so that we can have guidance for correcting specific weaknesses and for retaining those elements that are clearly advantageous.

Q—What do the ocular measurements show?

A—The ocular measurements reveal involuntary reactions. They determine whether the package draws attention and holds attention. There is no use trying to find out whether a package has appeal, that is, whether the consumers react favorably to it, if they don't see it because the competitive packages draw and hold the attention.

Q—Why do you use accumulated information and how do you get that information?

A—We have considerable information on the preference and retention power of basic images, most of them geometric in nature, and of colors with specific identity from experimental projects that I directed for seven years, from 1935 to 1942. In the last ten years we have tested images and colors by using them as controls or decoys in field tests for clients. It would not be very practical to conduct a field test with several hundred consumers to determine the preference rating (appeal) of a circle or triangle, of a specific red or green, when we have ratings for these based on tests conducted with thousands of consumers. We provide the ratings on images and colors based on accumulated information at very little cost.

Q—Do you test selling copy as well as packages and ads?

A—We do when we have to in connection with a package or ad. We also test brand names.

Q—Do any of your clients submit competitive packages for testing?

A—Yes, they do. They want to know how their packages rate against competition.

Q—The name Color Research Institute does not seem to represent the actual activities and services of your organization. How come you have this name?

A—The name describes an important part of our services. Also, it has meaning to the general public. Because of the name and our work with color, we can conduct our tests on an unconscious level by approaching consumers, not as marketing research people, but on a basis of interest to them. My book, "How to Color-Tune Your Home," published by the same house as "Color Guide for Marketing Media" (Macmillan), is our basic bond with consumers, that is, the public. We have other types of literature of interest to the general public, which we use as means for conducting tests on an unconscious level.

"Display Is a Visual Medium for Influencing People."

Q—Why does not Color Research Institute design packages?

A—Designing is a specialized field all in itself. The primary requisites of package designing are imagination, creativity, originality and an understanding of the engineering aspects of packaging and techniques in producing clean-cut art. We need personnel with almost the opposite kind of abilities, training and background. We must maintain perfect objectivity in contrast to designers, who are generally by nature and training subjective. We deal with statistics and the analysis of statistics. However, we work co-operatively with some of the outstanding designers in the country. If we did designing ourselves, we would be in danger of losing our objectivity or impartiality. It would be like a doctor diagnosing his own illness or performing an operation on his own child.

Q—I have heard that packages and products created by some of the most noted designers have failed. How do you explain this?

A—A designer's creativity and originality are his greatest assets. Paradoxically, these are also his greatest faults because he often goes too far into the future and loses the public. People enjoy change, but are often shocked by drastic change. To be effective a design must be original. It must have a distinct character and specific identity. At the same time, it must appeal to the great majority of people who are not interested in design yet unconsciously they are influenced by it. Because a design is produced, and has to be, by individuals who by nature, education and conditioning are subjective, we must use objective marketing research to determine the effect the design has on typical or average consumers. A modern package is designed primarily for display. Display is a visual medium for influencing people. Obviously, the designs you have in mind did not influence people to buy. Our tests would have shown whether those designs would influence consumers to buy the products.

Q—Is it always necessary to have a field test with several hundred consumers in order to determine the marketing effectiveness of a package?

A—When a package or design is submitted for testing, that is for determining its marketing effectiveness, it first of all goes to the lab for ocular measurements to determine its visibility from the shelf, the brand name readability and how it guides the eyes, or holds attention (eye-movement test). If the package fails in the ocular tests, it is returned to the company with specific recommendations for redesigning. Also, as I mentioned before, we don't field test individual colors for products or packages or brand identifying images for which we have ratings based on accumulated information derived from tests conducted during the last twenty years. Often, ocular measurements, that is, visibility, readability and eye-movement tests plus image and color ratings, are sufficient for determining the marketing effectiveness of a package.

Q—In brief, what are the advantages of unconscious level testing over direct interviewing?

A—The basic advantage of unconscious level testing techniques over direct interviewing is that it enables us to get consumers' natural reactions. It makes possible for us to have testing conditions similar to that of a shopping situation in which the consumer is not at all conscious that she is influenced by the package. As I have already pointed out, the average consumer is not aware that the imagery, colors and design on the label or box influence her choice of brand. If an individual is made conscious of the package design, she no longer is a typical consumer but takes on the role of an art critic. The average person's art standards are generally different from his unconscious or real reactions.

"An Astute Analyst ... Can Be Misled by Depth Interviewing."

Q—*Is there only one way of testing on an unconscious level?*

A—There are three kinds of unconscious level tests conducted at Color Research Institute: association tests, indirect preference tests and retention tests. The association test reveals favorable and unfavorable consumer attitudes toward the package or product. The indirect preference test shows which package the consumers actually prefer without their being aware that we are interested in their preference. The retention test measures the extent of recall of the package, ad, label or trademark. Each type of unconscious level test is conducted by integrating it with a subject of interest to the consumers in the test.

Q—*What evidence is there that CRI testing techniques are reliable?*

A—At this stage there should be no question about the reliability of our testing techniques. In the last ten years we have had many well-known marketing successes. The fact that marketing successes follow our favorable research reports is the best evidence.

MOTIVATION RESEARCH

Q—What evidence do you have that depth interviewing is not reliable? After all, Dr. Dichter has been very successful with depth interviews.

A—We have much evidence about the unreliability of depth interviewing and, as a matter of fact, we have evidence that even an astute analyst like Dr. Dichter can be misled by the depth interviewing technique. Both Dr. Dichter and Color Research Institute were employed to make a study of the marketing effectiveness of a trademark image in the form of a beautiful little girl and of an advertising campaign featuring the little girl with certain movie stars. Dr. Dichter's tests and our tests showed almost identical results on the movie stars. On the little girl, however, Dr. Dichter arrived at conclusions exactly the opposite from ours. His depth interviewers found, I was told, that consumers were not sufficiently familiar with the little girl as symbolizing the brand and that consumers did not believe that the little girl was real. He recommended not using this little girl as a trademark. However, our test, conducted on an unconscious level, showed that this little girl had the greatest number of favorable associations and fewer than 2 per cent unfavorable associations.

Q—What did this company do about the contradictory reports?

A—The fact that the little girl is used as a trademark very successfully provides the answer.

Q—What kind of company was this?

A—This company sells food products.

97

Q—Would you say that your tests are as reliable as point-of-sale testing?

A—Point-of-sale tests are first of all too costly to be called tests in the true sense of the word. Another important weakness in point-of-sale testing is that such a test shows which is the best of two or three, or any given number of packages. It does not show what makes one package weak and the other strong and it does not show that the strong package is the best possible marketing tool. Our tests pinpoint the weak points and the strong ones on a package. A CRI test-ratings report includes measurements of visibility from the shelf, brand name readability, attention-holding power, plus preference, association and retention ratings of the colors and the imagery. And in addition, our field tests show clearly how consumers react unconsciously or naturally to the package as a whole. Since there are other factors in marketing in addition to the package, a new brand or product has to be put into a regional market or test market. However, to be assured of an effective package, the package design should be put through Color Research Institute tests. A point-of-sale test could never reveal about the package what a CRI report shows.

Q—Can you always predict the success of a product on the basis of tests of the package and for what types of products have you made predictions?

A—After we conduct all the ocular and psychological tests and if all of them show that the package for a high quality product is optically and psychologically effective, I do not hesitate to predict and to state in writing that the product will have a great increase in sales, if all other marketing factors remain about the same. I have predicted the success of all sorts of products based on our tests of the packages—soap, detergents, toiletries, cigarettes, margarine, shortening, coffee, flour mixes, dog food, dishes, cooking utensils, sweepers, kitchen appliances, textiles and many other products.

"An Effective Package Is Next in Importance Only to the Product Itself."

Q—Is changing the package to a more effective one the only way of increasing sales?

A—Not at all. If a company will throw several million dollars into a promotion, it can increase the sale of a brand with the poorest type of package. However, getting an effective package is the more economical way and the most practical for getting a substantial increase in the market. Topnotch designers of packages charge large fees, but in the long run their fees are minor expenditures in comparison with the results that effective packages bring. For example, Philip Morris spent about a quarter of a million dollars on a packaging program. The success of Marlboro and the potential increase in sales of Philip Morris much more than justified the packaging expenditures. Of course, I want to add that the clever advertising idea used by Philip Morris— "Pardon us while we change our dress"—plus the very effective illustration, made an important contribution to the success of Philip Morris. However, without an effective package, the ad could never have maximum effectiveness.

Q—Which do you consider more important, the package or advertising?

A—This is like asking which is more important, day or night. However, the most popular talk I give is called, "The Four P's of Profit." The first P is product. A quality product is the first essential for an effective marketing program. The second P is the package. An effective package is next in importance only to the product itself, because the consumer unconsciously transfers the effect from the package to the product. In psychology we call this "sensation transference." The third P is promotion or advertising. Effective advertising is, of course, of great importance, but too often advertising people fail to realize that they can have effective advertising only if they have an effective package to advertise. The fourth P is price. Price in some cases has to be competitive. In other cases, price depends on numerous psychological factors, such as quality or prestige associations, practical application, etc. We should also be aware of the fact that the package remains on the shelf, whereas an ad is a one shot deal. The shopper is confronted with the package on the shelf in the aisle of the supermarket. She may not even see the ad even if she does read the magazine in which it appears.

Q—What happens to your prediction of the success of a package if the advertising is not effective?

A—That has actually happened. Twice I had to withdraw my forecast for a great increase in sales because it was evident to us that the advertising was poor.

Q—How did you know that the ads were not good?

A—We use many ads as controls in testing other ads and in this way we found that the ads of the clients for whom we predicted success with their new packages were too weak. In one case the ad was actually detrimental. We reported that to the client. This has not endeared me to the agency but I am not interested in winning popularity contests.

". . . Psychology Is Neither More nor Less Exact than Any Other Science."

Q—How long have you been conducting tests?

A—We started testing packages in 1945 when Color Research Institute was established as a marketing research organization. However, I started experimenting with tests as far back as 1935 when I took charge of several experimental projects in connection with the Adult Education Program of the Chicago Board of Education. On these projects we accumulated a great deal of information on colors, images and research techniques. This information became the basis for the procedures and techniques that are used at Color Research Institute.

Q—Have you ever made any wrong predictions about a package?

A—To my knowledge, no! If the advertising program is right, or at least if it is not detrimental and if there are no major changes in the marketing picture, a package that proves itself to be effective in all our tests will without question be effective in the market.

Q—Did you ever lose a client because of working with a competitive company?

A—No. I don't think we ever did. Our clients know that we are completely objective. Also, competitive companies are not handled by the same personnel. All our reports are confidential. The fact that our old clients continue working with us shows that they are not dissatisfied.

Q—Alfred Politz indicated that motivation research is not an exact science. Would you say that your type of research is an exact science?

A—There is no such thing as an exact science. Physics, chemistry and biology are no more exact sciences than psychology. When I was a boy I learned how many elements there were. Since then many new elements have been discovered. Cause and effect were considered absolute and not many centuries back gravity was considered something that could not be mastered by man. There are no absolutes any more. There is no exact science and psychology is neither more nor less exact than any other science. A scientific method means an objective method. We get information on consumers' attitudes from association tests and indirect preference tests. By obtaining spontaneous and natural responses from consumers, we learn their unconscious or subconscious reactions.

Q—I understand there were more than 100 package designs tested for Philip Morris?

A—Yes, there were, but all of them were not tested in the field. Only four reached the point of field testing.

Q—How did the four designs differ?

A—Basically, the four designs differed in that one had an oval as a brand identifying image, another a diamond, the third a shield and the fourth a modified oval. The package with the modified oval had by far the greatest number of favorable associations. Needless to say, the design with the modified oval was adopted. Some of the field tests were with the packages having the Philip Morris name on them and some without the Philip Morris identity. The tests showed very little difference in the consumer attitudes between the packages with the Philip Morris name on them and the packages with the name "greeked-in." In other words, these tests showed conclusively that consumers disliked the old dark brown package but that they like the Philip Morris name.

Q—Do you predict an increase in sales for Philip Morris cigarettes because of the new package?

A—On the basis of these tests, I believe Philip Morris has reason to expect a boost in sales of 25 per cent to 50 per cent—if other marketing factors remain the same. We tested the new ad and found it, as I said before, to be very effective. The advertising will, of course, play an important role in the success of Philip Morris.

Q—I understand that there were also more than 100 designs for the Marlboro package?

A—Yes, there were. Eight of these were selected for field testing because they rated very high in the visibility, brand name readability and in eye-movement tests. These eight designs were put through association tests. Finally, the number of package designs were narrowed to two, one design had a picture of a filter tip cigarette, the other a crest. In an association test with a sampling of 805 cigarette smokers, the design with the crest received over 80 per cent favorable associations. Marlboro management chose, of course, the basic package design with the crest image for its new pack. This is one of the most remarkable tests we have ever conducted. It shows that even a small detail like a crest can be very important in the consumer acceptance. Apparently, in the unconscious, or subconscious, the crest is associated by consumers with quality and prestige. Yet people can never tell you that they like a package or a product because they like the crest on it. It would not sound sensible.

Q—How about the colors on the Marlboro package. Why were they chosen?

A—The red is a high preference color and it also gives the package strong visibility. The black was chosen primarily because it has good readability. The brand name is emphasized in black.

Q—Is it true that before Marlboro introduced its new package the company had less than 1 per cent of the cigarette market and now it has 3 per cent of the total market and about 11 per cent of the filter market?

A—Yes, I believe this is true.

Q—Does the physical shape of the package have anything to do with the success of Marlboro?

A—The hard package has much to do with the success of Marlboro. This revolutionary type of package has tremendous appeal and the particular design created by Gianninoto is effective because of the physical character of the package. This type of design might not at all be an effective marketing device on a soft package.

Q—I hear that the success of some Lever Brothers products is due primarily to the use of foil. Do you think foil is a good thing to have for all packaging?

A—I think this is a very misleading idea. Good Luck margarine did not succeed because of the foil. There were a number of factors involved. The brand identifying image (the four leaf clover), the brand name and, of course, some marketing techniques were more important than the foil. The most important part of the success, I am sure, is due to the package, but not to the foil. You must keep in mind that this brand was successful before the foil was used. If there is one element that is more important than the others in the success of Good Luck margarine, it is the design and imagery of the four leaf clover. It is a remarkably effective marketing tool. In this case, foil contributed to the brand. However, foil can also be bad for a brand.

Q—Would you say that Lux could have kept its place

against the growing marketing competition without changing the package?

A—Yes, certainly, by throwing in several millions in promotion. However, making the package still more effective than it was, was more economical and more practical. I would not be surprised if sales have more than doubled since they put the new package on the market. It would have taken an awful lot of money to accomplish this by advertising the old package.

Q—You said that foil is not always good. But is it not commonly held by marketing people that the great success of Lux is really due to the foil?

A—This is sheer nonsense. There is a lot more than foil involved. The Lux design, which has been basically the same for many years, could easily be adapted to the gold foil. This cannot always be accomplished in a package change. The present Lux wrapper rates very high against the old wrapper, but there were several foil wrappers that did not do nearly as well in the tests as the old paper wrapper.

Q—Did any of the experimental wrappers tested for Lever use a crest?

A—No, I don't remember any wrapper with a crest, but I do remember one with a crown. A crown image has been found to be a very successful marketing device, yet on the experimental designs on foil for Lux soap it was a failure. This is an excellent example of the danger of generalizations. The crown can have a low preference rating and foil can have a low preference rating. It depends on the product, on the brand, on the design, on the specific problem.

Q—Do your tests show why a design is good or bad? Why is a crest or a crown effective?

A—Our research shows that often, certainly not always, a crest or a crown is effective as a marketing device. The research does not, and as far as we know, cannot show why. It shows only what is or is not effective. We can interpret or assume why, but we can not produce evidence. However, our clients are not interested in "why." They only want to know "what" is or is not effective.

Q—What evidence was there that the present Lux wrapper was effective?

A—Of four designs on foil, all of which were optically effective, the present Lux wrapper in gold foil with Lux in blue letters received the most favorable associations. In fact, rarely do we have a package that shows up so favorably in a field test. However, the other three wrappers, also in foil and optically effective, one having a crown, failed in the association tests.

Q—Can you tell me about the test that showed why the Good Luck margarine package is such a big success and did the change in the package coincide with the increase in sales?

A—Of course, the increase in sales coincided with the change in the package. I don't think there is any question about that. The Good Luck margarine package has had three major changes and it is well-known in marketing circles that each change meant an increase in sales.

Q—What specifically were those changes?

A—The original package had a brand identity weakness. It had a wonderful image of a four leaf clover, but the image was not played up. It played an insignificant role on the package. The first new package featured a piece of toast with a pat of margarine on it, but the four leaf clover was dominant as a brand identifying device. The next change was the silver foil and, here again, is an example showing that the use of foil is not a panacea. The design that was effective on paper or board showed up very poorly on foil. A new design had to be created to fit the new material. The company decided to drop the appetite appeal—toast and margarine—because they wanted to give still more emphasis to the brand identifying image, which they knew had remarkable effectiveness. The third change, which is now in use, puts even more emphasis on the four leaf clover. The four leaf clover is now three dimensional. Perhaps, I should add at this point, that the agency's contribution to the success of Good Luck margarine should not be minimized.

Q—What other services does Color Research Institute render besides testing packages and advertising matter?

A—Another of our services is providing color plans based on optical and psychological data for commercial and industrial interiors.

Q—Well, in summing up, how would you say we can

find out whether a foil wrap will increase sales for a product or whether a certain color will mean an increased share of the market or whether a specific shape or design is an effective marketing tool?

A—I can give you one answer to all these questions. By testing—first to determine how effective the package is optically and then determining how consumers react to it psychologically by means of controlled tests conducted on an unconscious level.

HOW TO PREDICT PACKAGING
SUCCESS

Food Business—January 1955

C H A P T E R 7

THERE'S no need to guess or worry about the marketing effectiveness of your package. Scientifically controlled tests, optical and psychological, in addition to objective market observations, make it possible to predict consumer reactions to any given container.

Such tests enabled us to forecast in 1952 the success of the then untried Betty Crocker cake mix and Good Luck margarine cartons. They also permit us to prophesize that a brand of dog food, not yet on the market, will be a great hit.

Each Component Measured

Scientific testing is accomplished by measuring the effect of each specific component of the package, and the package as a whole. The basic components are imagery, color, and pattern. The important image is the brand identifying symbol. The important color is the brand identifying one. The pattern is the overall design.

When testing and analyzing a package, we first find out three things about the image and the color: (1) How many people react favorably to them; (2) how great an impact they make on the memory; and (3) whether the image (a common circle, oval or triangle, or a complex trademark) and the color produce favorable, or unfavorable, associations with the product or its use.

This information is often derived from data accumulated in the course of tests involving more than 30,000 individuals with one color or image. On the basis of the available information we frequently determine the marketing value of the specific images and specific colors on packages, wrappers, labels, etc.

Then we test the optical effect of the package, by means of ocular-mechanical instrument measurements. Ocular measurements reveal involuntary reactions and show what the consumers see, how they read, and how they look at a design. They do not show psychological reactions. Nor do they reveal consumer attitudes or indicate consumer acceptance. A package, label, or ad must be "optically effective" before it can be "psychologically effective." The optical effectiveness is measured in terms of visibility from the shelf, readability, and eye-movement.

We use instruments for measuring how consumers look at a design. Optical sensations and reflexes are normally the same in all human beings. But, because eyesight varies with individuals, the tests are conducted with three to six persons. If three of them react in the same way, we conclude that others look at this pattern in the same way.

After we learn that the design as a whole is "optically effective" we proceed to determine its "psychological effectiveness." That is, we determine the consumers' attitudes to the design, which encompass a diversity of unconscious or subconscious, as well as some conscious associations.

A person's attitude toward an object is determined by many factors—including childhood environment, education, experience, economic status, libido, ego-involvement, prestige-identification, fetishes, phobias —with some of the factors in conflict with each other. Therefore, we must test at least four or five hundred individuals on an unconscious level before we can conclude how consumers will react.

Association-type field tests are used by Color Research Institute for measuring consumers' attitudes. The association tests are integrated with consumers' interests. They get spontaneous responses. They bring forth unconscious, uninhibited, unguarded reactions, which are like consumers' reactions in the store.

We generally do not have field tests at the beginning. First we take advantage of the accumulated information on colors and imagery. Then we conduct ocular measurements to determine visibility from the shelf, brand name readability, and eye-movement (how the package design guides the eyes).

Often, ocular measurements plus color and image ratings are all we need for ascertaining the marketing effectiveness of a new package design or of an old package or label.

However, sometimes a field test is necessary for one or more of the following reasons: A new design has imagery for which we have no ratings. Two or more new designs have equally high color and image ratings and equally good optical measurement ratings. Occasionally, the association of a color with a specific product has to be determined because we have no color association rating for the particular product. In all such cases, we conduct an association-type field test with from 400 to 1,200 consumers. The association test reveals consumers' attitudes (favorable and unfavorable).

The usual procedure for determining the marketing effectiveness of a package is the following:

A client sends to Color Research Institute his entire line of packages and the packages of major competition for a test-ratings and analysis report, which consists of ocular measurements (visibility, readability and eye-movement) and image and color ratings (preference, retention, and association) for each package in the line and for each competitive package.

When the image and color ratings and the ocular measurements are completed, they come to me for analysis and recommendations.

Possible Recommendations

The recommendations may be any of the following:

1. The image and color ratings and the ocular measurements show that all the packages in the line are effective marketing tools and should, therefore, be left as they are.

2. The image and color ratings show that the packages have minor weaknesses in imagery or in color. We recommend modifying the image or color, changing the image or color, or eliminating a specific element.

3. The visibility measurement ratings show that the following packages are lacking in visibility. It means the packages lack display power. They do not catch the consumer's eye as much, or as often, as they should. The visibility can be increased by doing thus: (We specify.)

4. The readability measurements show that the brand name readability should be improved by simplifying or enlarging the lettering.

5. The eye-movement test-ratings show that the following packages, or all the packages, in this line do not hold attention—that a competent designer should be employed to redesign the packages.

If the recommendation is any of those from No. 2 to No. 5, (not No. 1), the corrected, or modified, or new design is sent to Color Research Institute for ocular measurements—visibility from the shelf, brand name readability, and eye-movement tests.

If the image and color test-ratings and ocular measurement ratings are not conclusive for the reasons already given, we conduct a field test with from 400 to 1200 consumers.

The Betty Crocker packages, the Good Luck margarine package and hundreds of other packages have been put through this scientifically controlled testing procedure. Marketing results prove that packaging success is predictable.

THE IMPORTANCE OF COLOR ON INDUSTRIAL PACKAGES

Industrial Packaging—November 15, 1955

CHAPTER 8

I HAVE already written much about the importance of effective color, appropriate imagery and significant design in packaging of consumer products. The emphasis has generally been on food and toiletries.

Color Research Institute has prescribed colors and images, based on unconscious level tests conducted with consumers, for many retail store packages that are marketing successes.

Now I am asked whether color is an important factor in industrial packaging.

I can best answer this question by first analyzing why color, when applied on the basis of optical principles and psychological findings, is an effective marketing tool.

Color has always been with us and colors have always had an effect on people. But few individuals were aware of the effect that colors had on them. Generally, color was looked upon, and often still is, as a superficial frill.

COLOR ON INDUSTRIAL PACKAGES

Twenty years of color research has revealed many facts about color. We have learned much about the optical aspects of color and psychological tests have revealed much about the effect that colors have on people.

Although we occasionally hear individuals express strong likes and dislikes for certain colors, the impact of color sensations usually remains unconscious. People are not often aware that colors have a tremendous influence on them. They seldom realize that a person may be unconscious of the colors before him and yet be powerfully affected by them with regard to mood and behavior.

Most significant is the fact that color combinations that prove to have the greatest appeal in psychological tests are colors that are physically and optically balanced. However, color preference is complex because it is affected by many factors, among which are childhood environment, education and experience, with some of the factors in conflict with each other. Therefore, we must test at least four or five hundred individuals on an unconscious level, before we can conclude how consumers will react to a color or color combination or to an object in a specific color.

Extensive motivation research conducted by Color Research Institute has shown that sensation transference is an important factor in marketing. Sensation transference is the reason why an attractive store draws customers, why a beautiful automobile is considered a good car, why an effective package sells a brand. In other words, if the consumer has pleasant sensations

117

from the color of an auto, she or he is most likely to conclude that the car is of good quality; the sensation from the color is transferred to the performance of the car without consciousness of this fact.

Rarely is the consumer aware that he or she is influenced by the color (or design) of a product or package. Actually, the average consumer does not know what influences him. Generally the consumer wants to give the impression that she or he is logical or practical, whereas in reality she or he is behaving emotionally.

Large corporations have been built with the aid of effective symbolism of imagery and color. Colors (and images) with favorable symbolism promote a product, a brand, a company. Wrong symbolism often keeps a company from making progress. It can ruin a business and often does.

As I have already pointed out, colors always produce sensations but rarely does the average individual have a full conception of the effect that a color (or design) has on him.

Sensations involve associations which are generally unconscious or subconscious. These associations should be recognized as favorable or unfavorable symbolism. Some colors express "high quality," some denote "mediocrity" or "low quality."

The service station sign or trademark of the Standard Oil Company of Indiana is an outstanding example of effective symbolism. The colors are red, white and blue. These suggest that it is an American product. Also, the sign has a torch, which symbolizes a flame, oil.

Both the color and the image symbolism, which are with a small percentage of individuals conscious but with most people unconscious, are major factors in the company's successful marketing program.

In addition to the favorable colors and image symbolism, the shape of the sign, an oval, is a great asset. An oval has high preference and great appeal on a purely unconscious level.

One of the most important requisites in building a business or for establishing a product on the market is developing brand identity. Both color and imagery can be identity building devices. An effective trademark generally incorporates both high preference imagery and high preference color. The objective of the trademark is to get consumers used to seeing the image and associating it with the product. I want to point out here that a high preference color or image is one that has favorable unconscious and/or conscious associations or at least no negative or unfavorable associations.

Trademark Images

The trademark with the greatest retention power is the best brand identity builder. Some images, some colors can be easily recognized. They linger in the memory for a long time. Other colors and images lack retention power. They are seen and are immediately or soon forgotten. They do not make an impression on the mind and do not remain in the memory.

Tests have shown that some colors add to the retention power of an image. For example, a triangle is an image that can be easily recalled. An oval also rates high in recall. However, neither a triangle nor an oval (in black or white) remains in the memory as long as a triangle or an oval in black on yellow or black on orange or on red.

Yellow is seen from a greater distance than any other color. It catches the attention before any other color does. It is retained in the memory longer than any other color. Psychologically speaking, it "grows" in the memory.

Most blues, on the other hand, are not seen at a great distance. They do not attract attention. They easily escape from the mind. The effect from blue shrinks or evaporates. That is why we say that blue has low retention, whereas yellow and orange-red have high retention ratings.

However, yellow rates low in preference. It appeals to few people, whereas blue generally rates high in preference. Both strong retention power and high preference are essential marketing factors.

Choosing a Color

Because no color has both, very high preference and very strong retention in the memory, choosing a color or colors for a package or product is difficult. There are still many other factors, one of which is the association of the color with the particular product or its use.

COLOR ON INDUSTRIAL PACKAGES

For example, some reds are favorably associated with "food," with "cooking" and with "kitchen." Other reds have negative associations with these words. Most, but not all, blues rate very high in association with "hardware," but they rate very low when they are associated with "cosmetics."

Then there are factors such as the quantitative aspect, amount of color or size or area, and color combinations. Some color combinations produce favorable associations. Other combinations bring forth unfavorable sensations. The legibility or readability power of color is also a factor in marketing.

Thus, it becomes evident that generalizations about color are dangerous. There is no absolute standard in color and design. Each color and design problem is unique. Each involves specific optical aspects and psychological factors.

There are no "experts" in color or design who can tell us how consumers will react to a particular color combination or to a design. Each color, each combination, each design has a distinctive ocular pattern and a totally different psychological effect from any other combination of colors and images.

That is why only through marketing research can we get the answer to how consumers will react to a color or design. Research can tell us which of a number of designs or colors is the most effective marketing tool and which is not. However, not all so-called research can do this.

Consumer expressions of real preferences and true attitudes are revealed by testing on an unconscious level. Testing marketing media on an unconscious level means having test conditions in which there are no defense mechanisms playing a part. Testing on an unconscious level means using indirect methods to get actual preferences that involve self-interest or getting natural, spontaneous, consumer reactions that reveal true attitudes.

What Some Companies Did

Consoweld laminates are an excellent example of scientific color use. The hues for the Consoweld surfacing materials were chosen on the basis of a color system derived from the visible spectrum. The specific tones were chosen on the basis of psychological tests (of the association type) with consumers. Also, the patterns were chosen on the basis of unconscious level tests with consumers. By approaching its marketing problem scientifically, the Consoweld Corporation achieved two objectives (which some people consider unattainable)—(1) of limiting the number of colors and patterns, thus keeping the inventory at a minimum and (2) of more than doubling business in a short time.

To some, perhaps I should say to many, limiting colors and patterns means limiting sales. Not so to the men who conduct the business of the Consoweld Corporation. These men did not try to guess what color and pattern Mrs. X wants on her kitchen counter, on her bathroom wall, on her breakfast table or on her cocktail table. Nor did they consult their wives. They used reliable research and they got reliable answers. They knew how to interpret and make use of the information that evolved from research.

Bissell sweepers are another outstanding example. "Experts" said the day of the non-electric sweeper is gone. Bissell Carpet Sweeper Company executives were not influenced by the predictions of doom. They went out looking for reliable research. From research they learned that "right colors" will boost sales. Through research they obtained the "right colors." The Bissell Carpet Sweeper Company has been doing very well, indeed.

A number of companies in the kitchen appliances field went into color. It seems that some merely jumped into a mass of color. Other companies used research. They chose each of their colors on the basis of unconscious level tests with consumers. They are free to concentrate on manufacturing, promotion programs and on distribution problems. They know they have the right colors.

We should always remember that the right color on the product itself is not all there is to using color as an effective marketing tool. The carton in which the product is shipped is a vital factor in the total picture of company success. One carton says to the unconscious mind: "This carton contains a valuable object, a beautiful thing, an article of quality." Another carton suggests to the unconscious mind: "This is an inferior article, I wish I had bought a better one."

The color on company trucks plays an important role in marketing. One truck says to the unconscious mind of the pedestrian before whom the Sunbeam Bread truck passes, this is Sunbeam Bread, "This is the famous Sunbeam Bread, this is the high quality bread." These favorable sensations rarely become conscious, but they have a tremendous effect on the unconscious mind, thus influencing the attitude of the consumer.

Another truck crosses the street in front of the same pedestrian. This truck is merely a dangerous vehicle. It brings forth no favorable associations. It has an unfavorable effect on the unconscious mind.

Colors (and designs) are very important factors in industrial packaging because colors play major roles, not only in the home, but wherever they are seen, on cartons, on trucks, on railroad cars, on passenger trains.

Sometimes colors play favorable roles and other times unfavorable roles. Always we should remember that the effects of colors (and designs) are on the unconscious mind. The consumer is rarely aware that the color says, "I am covering a cheap, unreliable mechanism," or "I look cheap because what I cover is cheap."

Research, conducted on an unconscious level, has shown that the right color is not always bright, nor is it always dull. The right color is not always pure nor is it always neutral. Color appropriateness depends on many factors only some of which are brought out in this short article.

COLOR ON INDUSTRIAL PACKAGES

Research conducted on an unconscious level tells us which color (which design) says to the unconscious mind of the consumer: "I am quality," "I give happiness," "I am safe," "I make you feel at ease," "I make you feel relaxed," "I should belong to you."

WHY YOU MUST TEST YOUR
PACKAGE DESIGN

Canadian Packaging—November 1955

CHAPTER 9

If You're In Packaging, Then You're Too Close
To Judge It Fairly

TESTS show that the more conscious one is about packaging, the further away he is from the reactions of the typical consumer. The more knowledge one has about packaging design the less he behaves like the average shopper.

When I go to the supermarket, I look at packages. To me, the packages are the important elements in the store. To the other shoppers, if they don't happen to be designers, the packages are merely containers with brand identifications. "Normal" shoppers give no thought to packaging designs. They are hardly ever conscious that packages are designed.

The designer is a little further away from the typical consumer than is the marketing research man. He is not only consciously trying to find out the effect that a package may have, but he is also concerned with such factors as design, style, technique and reproduction media. I saw one man in a supermarket examining a can, trying to see whether the can was lithographed in two, three or four colors. Another "expert," whose home I visited, removed the label from a can to see whether it was reproduced in letterpress or offset.

The average consumer is not concerned with the aesthetics of the package, nor with the technicalities of producing it. She is not consciously bothered by the psychological aspects of the package. She is not aware that there are any psychological elements in the grocery store. I cannot trust my reactions to a package. That is, I cannot permit myself to consider my reactions as typical of the average consumer because my background is not typical, my conditioning and my education are not typical of the average shopper.

Having seen many reports of tests on how average consumers generally react to specific patterns, I know that they do not react as I do, or rather that I do not react as they do. We don't always know why consumers react as they do, but from Psychoanalysis we have learned some of the factors that influence attitudes.

What Affects Consumers?

A person's attitude toward an object is determined by many factors. Childhood environment is one important factor that influences an individual's attitude toward an object. Type of education is another important

127

element. The libido, or the natural drive for pleasure, is weak in one individual, very strong in another.

There are people who have fetishes. One woman I know has a "green" fetish. She will buy anything in a green package.

Another housewife I met has a number of phobias. Among her phobias are triangles. She won't look at anything that has a triangle on it. No matter how good a brand is, she won't buy it if there is a triangle on the package.

We have a record of one housewife whose fetish is rounded forms. She keeps at least three dozen boxes of salt and many cans of shortening and coffee in her cupboard. The reason is that she loves round containers. Products that come in rectangular containers she buys only one at a time. Yet she is more like the typical consumer than a trained researcher or an experienced designer.

Another woman I know despises yellow. She has a hard time finding white margarine. She says that she is not going to pay for the coloring matter. She can't afford it, but she can afford T-bone and sirloin steaks for dinner nearly every day. Many individuals have all sorts of phobias.

There is, of course, the "economic status" of the consumer. Economic factors are not all economical; they are also psychological. Take for example the woman who did not want the margarine in the metal foil package because the "silver costs too much." The prices were marked. The foil package was marked 2 cents less than the yellow package without foil. Shoppers often see what they want to see, what they have been conditioned to see.

There are also ego-involvement and prestige identification factors in the store. This is where advertising and brand prestige play important roles. The highly advertised brand has prestige. It gives the housewife ego-satisfaction. She feels she is buying the best-known brand. Best-known is associated with and identified as best quality.

The Price Factor

Higher price enters into this picture because it is often identified with higher quality. Cheaper means both cheaper in quality and cheaper in price to many a consumer.

Imagery on the package also plays an important role in prestige identification and ego-involvement. For example, tests have shown that the crest on a package of cigarettes is associated with high quality and prestige by the consumer. A crown image brings forth prestige associations in the unconscious or subconscious mind.

Of course, all consumers do not have the same experiences. They do not have the same backgrounds, nor do they always have similar education. They do not have the same emotional makeup. They differ in their behavior patterns. That is why we must test with several hundred consumers in order to approximate the typical consumer.

But, "normal" or average consumers have one thing in common, they give no conscious importance to the package of a product. In this they are unlike the marketing specialist. In this they are completely different from the research person or the package designer.

Extensive motivation research conducted by Color Research Institute has shown that sensation transference is an important factor in marketing. Sensation transference is the reason why an attractive store draws customers, why a beautiful automobile is considered a good car, why an effective package sells a brand.

In one test, 86 per cent of the women wanted one of three coffees because it was the best. Actually all three coffees were the same, only the containers differed. In another test, 99 per cent of a group of women claimed a pat of white butter "tasted oily like margarine" and a pat of yellow margarine "tasted like butter." These are examples of transference of an optical sensation to a taste sensation. Sensation transference from the package to the contents is a common occurrence in the supermarket. That is why the package is such an important factor in marketing.

Tests show that the average consumer does not know what influences him. Because he doesn't know, he can't tell you. That is why marketing research must be conducted on an unconscious level.

"Testing marketing media on an unconscious level" means having test conditions in which there are no ego-involvement and prestige identification factors and in which no defense mechanisms play a part. Testing on an unconscious level means using indirect methods to get actual preferences that involve self-interest or getting natural spontaneous consumer reactions that reveal true attitudes.

Top-notch designers are specialists who are trained in producing original designs. They are able to conceive original concepts, significant imagery and meaningful patterns. They have the imagination and skill to create new designs on the basis of design principles that may arouse the emotions of men and women.

But designers are not able to determine whether the average individual in the store will be attracted by the package—whether he or she will react in favor of or against the package design. Nor are research specialists who are trained in techniques of testing in a position to predict without benefit of testing the effect a new package will have on consumers.

The scientifically trained mind uses logical and deductive thinking. Designers often are logical and scientific in their methods in developing a package design.

But logic and deductive thinking are not a reliable basis for putting a package on the market. The marketing process is not logical but is dependent on consumers' emotional reactions. Consumer reactions to a complex visual unit—pattern or design—cannot be predetermined by logic or deduction.

One of the very best designers was working on a package for a new filter tip cigarette. He reasoned that, since this is a new brand of filter tip, the logical thing to do is to show a realistic illustration of a filter tip cigarette on the front panel of the package. At the same time, he also produced another package identical in design but with one difference, instead of a filter tip cigarette, he put a crest on the front panel.

Both packages were put through an association-type test by Color Research Institute. The test showed that the "logical" package with the filter tip cigarette image was associated with low quality and had a predominance of other unfavorable associations. The one with the crest image was associated with high quality and had a predominance of other favorable associations. This is an excellent example of a top-notch designer's logic not being indicative of favorable consumer reaction. This designer was aware of the value of research. He welcomed having a number of his designs submitted for unconscious level testing.

The following case shows how a research analyst's deduction was wrong. Research conducted on an unconscious level shows that triangles do not have feminine appeal. A triangle has a very low percentage of favorable associations, presumably because of the sharp points. When two triangles are combined into one image, it should from a logical point of view, be as bad, or nearly twice as bad. It should be expected to have about twice as many negative associations or at least as many negative associations as a single triangle, the research analyst reasoned.

However, when the double triangle was tested with a large sampling of consumers in association-type tests, it was revealed that to a great majority of consumers the double triangle has no relationship to a triangle. It is a diamond. As such, it has a high percentage of favorable associations and a low percentage of unfavorable associations.

In other words, an image produces a specific effect which cannot be accurately translated into the effect that would be produced by another image, no matter how similar the two images are.

This is why at Color Research Institute we don't give opinions. We don't make judgments without the support of research. We are not "experts" who can tell by looking at a design whether it will be an effective marketing tool.

Only by testing can anyone find out how effective a package will be as a marketing tool. Testing, remember, does not mean interviewing consumers because consumers cannot tell us what influences them because they are affected by sensation transference. Nor do we mean point-of-sale testing. There are a number of tests conducted at Color Research Institute before the package is produced for delivery to a market. These tests are controlled. At the point of sale there can hardly ever be reliable controls.

A point-of-sale test can show only failure or success. The controlled testing procedure we follow reveals specific weaknesses and strengths of the package.

At Color Research Institute each package is first put through ocular measurements—to reveal consumers' involuntary reactions to the package. The ocular measurements are a visibility test, brand name readability test and an eye-movement test.

Then the imagery and colors of the package or design are given ratings. These are based on accumulated statistical data derived from indirect preference and association-type tests conducted with thousands of consumers over the past twenty years.

If the package has on the front panel an image that rates low in preference, retention or association or it has a dominant color with low preference and unfavorable associations, the design gets a negative report. If the design receives favorable color and image ratings, but gets a low visibility rating, a poor brand name readability rating, or it fails in the eye-movement test, recommendations for redesigning are made.

If, however, the design has imagery and colors that rate high in preference, in retention in the memory and in favorable associations and the design has sufficient visibility, good brand name readability and it guides the eyes smoothly, it means that the package gets a favorable test-ratings report.

However, sometimes a field test is necessary for one or more of the following reasons: A new design has imagery for which we have no ratings. Two or more new designs have equally high color and image ratings and equally good ocular measurement ratings. Occasionally, the association of a color with a specific product has to be determined because Color Research Institute has no color association rating for the particular product. In all such cases, we conduct an association-type field test with from 400 to 1,200 consumers. The association test reveals consumers' attitudes (favorable and unfavorable).

This is a scientifically controlled testing procedure. This is how we can make sure that a package will be an effective marketing tool.

Research specialists are trained in testing techniques. They cannot judge the effectiveness of a package without the benefit of testing. They must conduct tests under strictly controlled conditions. Designers are specialists in creating packages. They cannot predict on the basis of consumers' reactions. Consumers themselves cannot tell how they are affected by a package because they actually do not know.

By testing on an unconscious level (by means of controlled tests that reveal consumers' involuntary reactions and by tests that bring out unconscious reactions to the package) we learn whether the package is an effective marketing tool.

Each package design is by nature and purpose different from every other package design. Human reactions to colors, images and patterns cannot be determined through logic or deduction.

Only by testing consumer reactions on an unconscious level can we learn the marketing effectiveness of a package. Often tests have shown that a slight change in a package drastically altered consumer attitudes to the package. Frequently packaging changes had no effect on the consumer whatever, yet the change was significant to the design-educated eye.

THE INSIDE STORY ABOUT
THE LITTLE ELVES

U. S. News Bulletin—March 1955

CHAPTER 10

HERE is the story of the New Teenie Weenie label for canned food products of the Oconomowoc Canning Company.

A statement by J. B. Weix, Oconomowoc Canning Company: "We believe you will be interested in the story of how we developed the Teenie Weenie labels, as reprinted from the U. S. News Bulletin, a publication of the United States Printing & Lithograph Company. It is our aim to provide our distributors who feature our controlled brands with labels that are optically and psychologically tested and market proven to do a thorough merchandising and selling job for our products. We, also, believe that our distributors who are using their own brands will be interested in our experiences in producing this successful label."

INSIDE STORY ABOUT LITTLE ELVES

Teenie Weenie Trade Characters Do Giant-Size
Job on New Labels for Oconomowoc
Canned Vegetable Packs

There is nothing "teeny" about the merchandising and selling job that the newly created Teenie Weenie trade characters are doing on the canned vegetable packs of the Oconomowoc Canning Company. In fact by all standards the new tiny elf twins are doing a man-size job of moving canned peas, corn and beans from retail store shelves.

The appealing elf-like trade characters, Teenie and Weenie, came into being as part of the packaging re-design project completed recently by U-S packaging designers. They were developed as a distinctive and easily recognizable trademark for Teenie Weenie brand products. In the short time they have been performing in retail food outlets, they have had a most satisfactory acceptance.

Two U-S design departments collaborated in the design project, working with James A. Gage, Milwaukee sales office, who handles the Oconomowoc account. The original designs, including the trade characters, were developed in the Cincinnati design department. All finished art work for the label was completed in the Chicago art department.

The Teenie Weenie twins have been so designed to lend themselves to prominent use on the display panel of the new labels, as well as in supporting advertising and store promotional material. The label design technique incorporates the prominent display of the products in the hands of elf twins, which tends to more closely associate the product with the brand name. As a result, not only is brand identification strengthened on the display panel of the label but, also, the identification of the particular product is faster.

On the consumer panel of the label, illustrated recipes have been replaced by the familiar Teenie Weenie twins and a repetition of the brand name. Also, included are instructions for preparation with copy emphasis on the "tender, fresh and tasty" qualities of the product—one of the important features of Teenie Weenie brand vegetables.

Design Pre-tested

Before final adoption, the new designs were pretested in the Chicago testing laboratories of the Color Research Institute. The test-ratings reports were unusually high and included not a single recommendation for change. In a covering letter with the report, addressed to the Oconomowoc Canning Company, the Color Research Institute had this to say:

"Enclosed is the report on the Teenie Weenie design. It may interest you to know that it is very rare for us to issue a test-ratings report that calls for no changes at all. We can find no weakness in the new design and recommend it unreservedly.

INSIDE STORY ABOUT LITTLE ELVES

"The designer should really be congratulated on a very effective job in creating a label that is a superior marketing tool."

As the new labels began appearing on the market, trade reaction was extremely favorable. Typical of some of the response was contained in a letter to officials of the Oconomowoc Canning Company from the Fred W. Albrecht Grocery Company.

In this letter it was reported that the sale of Teenie Weenie brand merchandise had increased three to four times since the use of the new label—and this increase without any special display or promotion, and without any special price.

Although the introduction of the new labels has been made to date without fanfare, additional promotional efforts are contemplated for the new 1955 packs. Even so, the initial impact of the new designs has had a marked effect which heralds great success for Teenie Weenie products under the trademark of the jolly twin elves.

Oconomowoc Canning Company   January 28, 1955
Oconomowoc, Wisconsin.

ATTENTION: MR. JOE WEIX

Dear Joe:

Whenever one of your customers finds a piece of glass, or worm, or leaf, or any foreign object in a can of peas or corn, you undoubtedly hear about it.

This is not one of those kind of letters. Yesterday, our manager, Charlie Eggers, from Acme #9 located in the Magic City Shopping Center in Barberton, Ohio, stopped in my office for a few minutes, and out of a "clear sky" told me that the new label on Teenie Weenie merchandise was doing a whale of a job for the product. I tried to pin Charlie down, and the best I could do was that—with no particular promotion, no special display and no special price, over a period of just a few weeks, the sales had gone from three or four cases each per week to ten to fifteen cases each per week.

Knowing Charlie as I do, I don't believe that he exaggerated it because, again with no special promotion on Teenie Weenie, he ordered out fifty cases of each, and is now going to see what the new label will do when it is prominently displayed.

It's always nice to know that any improvement in your product is noticed, and that it helps sales. That is the occasion of this letter. I am sure that some day, if you should find time to drop a short note to Manager Charlie Eggers, he would be delighted to hear from you—and one of these days we might be able to report a "real success story" on Teenie Weenie in Acme Market #9.

The best of luck to you in 1955.

Sincerely,

THE FRED W. ALBRECHT GROCERY COMPANY
M. F. Musser, Advertising Manager

MFM:ec

An Explanation of Color Research Institute Testing Techniques

In pre-testing the new Teenie Weenie design the Color Research Institute employed a laboratory technique. Here is a copy of the report and a brief statement of the test-rated elements involved.

INSIDE STORY ABOUT LITTLE ELVES

TEST-RATINGS OF NEW TEENIE WEENIE LABEL
as Contained in the Confidential Report of the Color Research Institute
of America

Report for Oconomowoc Canning Company, March 11, 1954
Teenie Weenie June Peas Design

COLOR AND IMAGE RATINGS

Test		Ratings
Color preference	—White	80-90
	—Red	88
	—Green	80
	—Yellow	34
Color retention	—White	85-95
	—Red	88
	—Green	78
	—Yellow	90
Color association	—Green—"peas"	85-100
Image preference	—Modified Oval	70-92
	—Elf Figures	No Rating
	—Peas	85-100
Image retention	—Modified Oval	85-86
	—Elf Figures	No Rating
	—Peas	85-100
Image association	—Modified Oval—"Teenie Weenie"	No Rating
	—Elf Figures —"Teenie Weenie"	No Rating
	—Peas —"peas"	100

OCULAR MEASUREMENTS

Visibility	—	88
Readability	—Teenie Weenie	84
	—June Peas	80
Eye-movement	—Eyes fell on *Teenie Weenie* where attention was held, moved to *June Peas* and then to peas at bottom of label where attention was held.	A (Excellent)

"No Rating" means Color Research Institute has no rating, that a field test would be necessary in order to get it.

Analysis

The ratings show that the new (No. 7) Teenie Weenie design is an effective marketing tool.

The design has an effective balance of high preference and high visibility colors.

The modified oval rates high as a marketing device. It has high prefer-ence, that is great appeal, and strong retention in the memory.

Although we have no ratings for the elf figures, we know, without con-ducting a special field test, that they have strong brand identity value and symbolize the brand very effectively.

The visibility of the label is very good.

The readability of the brand name is very good.

The design gets and holds attention, as is shown by the eye-movement test.

Recommendation

The ratings show that the label design has no specific weak aspects and adoption of the design, as it is, is recommended.

There are three basic ocular sensations—image, color and design (organization or arrangement of images and colors).

There are three aspects of each of these three ocular sensations that are important factors in marketing (nine elements):

Color—preference, retention, association.

Image—preference, retention, association.

Design—visibility, readability and eye-movement (attention-holding power).

By determining the degree of effectiveness of each of the nine elements, we learn the degree of effective-ness of the entire unit. We are thus also able to correct the specific weak elements and to retain the strong ones.

The test ratings of color preference, retention, asso-ciation and image preference, retention, association, are based on accumulated statistical information.

The test-ratings of visibility, readability and eye-movement are ocular-mechanical measurements of the actual designs.

NOW THEY'RE "PSYCHOANALYZING" ADVERTISING

By Bob Bergen
Los Angeles Mirror—March 1955

CHAPTER 11

A LOT has happened in this field since Louis Cheskin, director of Chicago's Color Research Institute, got interested in it in 1935.

It is now possible, for example, to give ads an eye-movement test. This is done with an ocular-mechanical device that charts the movements of a reader's eyes as he glances through the copy. It reveals where attention is held and where the eyes tend to skip.

If there's a blind spot, Cheskin says, there is something wrong with the make up.

Slogan "Staying Power"

Reader association, which involves consumer attitudes toward copy, also can be tested in advance. Consumers are asked to associate the ads with a list of favorable and unfavorable words. Associations with the unfavorable words reveal unfavorable attitudes before they can do any damage.

There also is a retention test that measures recall of the imagery, product and brand name. It shows what percentage of readers remember these three factors as well as, for example, the "staying power" of slogans.

Cheskin bases his approach on the premise that "it is the unconscious purpose rather than the reasoning process that generally determines how an individual will behave."

People, he says, forget much of their past. But these presumably "forgotten" experiences really aren't forgotten. They remain in the unconscious where they continue to exert tremendous power over the way people act.

Sensation Transference

Which, to Cheskin, means that market research based on the assumption that human beings will do what they say they will "is naive." Market research, in other words, must become motivation research. And here he gets into such things as sensation transference —the reason why an attractive store draws customers, a beautiful car is considered a good car, why an effective package sells a brand.

In one test he conducted, 86 per cent of the women involved wanted one of three coffees "because it is the best." Actually all the coffees were the same. Only the containers differed. It's an example, says Cheskin, of transference of an optical sensation to a taste sensation.

Only way to learn the real preference of a customer is by testing on the "unconscious level."

GIVE YOUR PACKAGES
"APPETITE APPEAL"

By John M. Tindall
Baking Industry—October 23, 1954

CHAPTER 12

Design and color of the package and its trademark condition consumers' attitudes toward
food products.

WRAPPING up a sale today is quite different from
what it was 45 years ago. We must be alert to do better
and meet today's needs because times have changed—
needs are different and will continue to change.

In merchandising, change from service stores to self-
service super markets, improved canning, freezing of
foods, better packaging of goods, better transportation,
bigger advertising campaigns, California and Florida
fresh fruits and vegetables in your favorite shopping
center only days later, air freight shipments with dew-
fresh merchandise daily at your favorite food store—
all denote improvements.

There is more competition now for the dollar. You
won't get your share if you are just engaged in a fight

for each other's business. Look at the man to the right of you, then look at the man to the left. In these times he is your partner, not your competitor. Why? Because bread has gained a negative reputation that it doesn't deserve because of food fads, special diets and the like. Here are several other reasons why bread sales have decreased: better availability of all types of foods, less physical exercise, and more balanced meals. Look at magazines, radio, and television. They are all selling appetite appeal. Your competitors are not bakers only, but manufacturers of other food, and all are after a greater share of the food dollar.

Increase Sales—Not Switch Sales

In this modern age our eyes turn to research and the science of things. Waxed paper manufacturers are dedicated to the task of selling more of everybody's bread, not to fostering competition between each of you for each other's business. Nor do they wish to create a sale for one item at the expense of another.

Why do I have the conviction that waxed paper makes an important contribution to the food distributor, the grocer, the consumer? I know the grocery business from the bottom up. I have watched thousands of consumers in my own grocery stores, and studied the psychological implications on consumers' reactions when they are in a grocery store. Is there factual information available on such reactions? Are there statistics on the kind of packages consumers buy? Why do consumers buy more of certain types of packages than of other types? Wanting evidence and more answers than I had, I decided to go where I could get answers to these questions.

Having heard of the work of the Color Research Institute in Chicago in the field of packaging, I contacted them and spent several days with Louis Cheskin, director of the institute. Mr. Cheskin confirmed the information I had, and showed me a wealth of data, reports on numerous tests, and a great number of case histories. He pointed out that no longer can we consider a package as merely a container to protect the product from damage, atmospheric conditions and transport hazards.

The Silent Salesman

In modern marketing, the package must be planned to convey the use of the contents. It must attract the consumer. It must arouse his imagination (really her imagination, because more than 80 per cent of shoppers are women). The package, to be an effective marketing tool, must provide an effective setting. It must be a silent salesman.

The final stage of a meal has appetite appeal, not the basic ingredient, Mr. Cheskin pointed out. Mouths do not water at the sight of raw meat or slices of bread. Children don't yell, "Goody! Goody!" when they see bread on the table. But men and women get a feeling of hunger when they look at a table attractively set with roasted brown meat, colorful vegetables, and fresh looking bread. Children cry, "Oh, boy!" when they get a slice of bread with butter and their favorite jam.

"In Asia and in many parts of Europe, the food product itself has fascination. Bread and meat or fish have no fascination for the American consumer. In this land of plenty the basic ingredients are largely taken for granted. The American housewife is primarily concerned with quality rather than quantity. She can normally get the quantity of food she needs and wants, but she is not always sure of the quality. By quality she means the final quality, the quality of taste, the quality that means enjoyment, the quality that means pleasure in eating appetizing food."

The Color Research Institute conducted a number of tests to determine how consumers react to foods. They used a "psychogalvanometer" (similar to a lie detector), several kinds of association-type tests and preference tests. The tests showed that well-fed Americans have no emotional response to raw meat, fish, eggs or bread. But the same consumers get quite excited when a charcoal-broiled steak is put before them, when an attractively garnished platter is placed before their eyes, when they view a sizzling plate of ham and eggs, when they see a jam or butter-covered slice of bread.

These tests demonstrated the fact that packages with appetite appeal are much more effective marketing tools than packages without appetite appeal.

The Color Research Institute does market-testing for numerous companies. The appetite appeal images were not put on their packages by accident. They are the result of extensive research with consumers.

I asked Mr. Cheskin this question: "I can see how people enjoy seeing a realistic picture of appetizing food, but how does such a picture sell the brand, that is, the product in the wrapper or carton?" He asked for a file on marketing tests and explained that design effect is generally on an unconscious level. Color becomes a conscious element only where ego-involvement and prestige identification are factors, such as in wearing apparel and interior decorating. The consumer is generally not aware that he or she is influenced by color or design. The tests demonstrated that consumers often thought one brand superior and another inferior; yet the only difference between the two was the color of the package.

Tests Reveal Transference

Tests from Color Research Institute files demonstrate that consumers cannot tell us what they like about a product. For example, a large number of women at a luncheon were asked whether they could differentiate between butter and margarine. Over 90 per cent said they preferred butter because margarine tasted "oily, greasy, more like shortening than butter."

Two pats were served—a yellow (margarine) and a white (butter). The ladies were asked whether they could discern any difference. The yellow pat (margarine) tasted like butter to 99 per cent of the ladies, but the white pat (butter) tasted oily like margarine. This demonstrated that people confuse sensations. The ladies attributed to the sense of taste the characteristics that belong to the sense of sight. It was a case of transference of an optical sensation to a taste sensation.

Another example is that of a well-known brand of detergent. The blue in the detergent is a very successful marketing device. Color also played a part in the detergent package. An identical design was produced in three color schemes. In the consumer tests one of the packages came out with the most favorable associations and highest preference. The second was not quite as effective. The third proved to be mediocre. Yet the designs were identical, except for the color.

Still other examples of the power of color in marketing are the following: The change of the dominant color of a label, one value of yellow to another, was mainly responsible for increased sales of a well-known gin. Changing the hue on the label for shortening boosted its sales. Changing the color of a cosmetic promoted its sales.

A client manufacturing a detergent wanted to know which of three package designs (each of which had a high average rating) had the greatest association with "strong" and "heavy duty." An association-type test revealed one package design had 60 per cent association with "strong" and "heavy duty." The second package design had a 37 per cent association. And the third had 13 per cent. The test showed conclusively which of the three package designs was the most effective for a heavy duty detergent.

Best Design for Food

For a food product, an association-type test showed that one package had a very high association with kitchen and cooking, another design had a fair association, and the third was associated with kitchen and cooking by only six out of a hundred. "People are rarely conscious of color, yet they are greatly affected by it," Mr. Cheskin said.

He pointed out clearly that sensation transference plays a major role in marketing. Unconsciously and consciously consumers are affected by color, abstract imagery, and realistic appeal imagery. This effect is transferred to the product or the brand. In other words, some colors and images suggest "strong," some suggest "weak." Some colors and images tell the subconscious or unconscious mind "good," some say "bad." Some colors and images tell the unaware consumer "mediocre." Some tell him or her "high quality," "delicious," or "healthful."

Brand Selling Too

But as a baker you are not interested in selling just any bread. You are interested in selling your bread. Appetite imagery sells bread but it does not mean that the imagery is necessarily identified with your brand of bread. Tests have shown that often the effect of an illustration is beneficial to the industry, but not specifically of greatest benefit to the brand. Your competition can also have appetite appeal imagery, which the consumer may confuse with the imagery on your package. You should, therefore, have on your package imagery that specifically identifies your brand only. Mr. Cheskin put great emphasis on the importance of imagery in brand selling.

Thus you require a brand-identifying image, in addition to appetite appeal imagery. Also important is a brand-identifying color. Brand-identifying images are often known as trademarks, and can be potent marketing devices. An effective trademark is one with strong appeal, that is easily recalled or recognized. It is still better if it has favorable association with the product or the use of the product.

The dominant color, or brand identifying color also must have high preference, easy retention in the memory and favorable associations for the package to be an effective marketing tool. Mr. Cheskin said, "Experience and reports on market tests showed wrong colors can ruin a package as a marketing tool, and right colors boost sales. Correct color use in merchandising means greatly increased sales because the right color gives a product greater preference, favorable association with the product or its use (appeal), greatly increased visibility (display) in the market place, and greater retention in the memory (recall)."

"However, the wrong use of color can be worse than no color at all. For example, tests have shown that clean light yellows, orange-reds, and browns have high preference ratings in association with foods, whereas some greens, cool reds, and many blues have low preference ratings in association with foods. Tests with consumers show a certain green to have the highest preference rating in association with jewelry, and the lowest preference rating with food products." Mr. Cheskin also pointed out that bright warm colors give the appearance of larger size.

"Colors are tested separately to determine how consumers are affected by the colors alone. The basic images, trademarks and/or illustrations are tested by themselves to learn to what degree they are effective in influencing consumers. Then the design, as a whole, is tested. Visibility is measured from the shelf. Readability of the brand name is determined. A measurement, called an eye-movement test, shows how the consumer looks at the package, where the eyes fall, what parts they skip, and whether the package gets and holds attention."

"A package design, an advertising page, a poster, a billboard, counter or window display are all governed by the same optical and psychological principles. Basically, all are different types of product displays. Display is defined as a visual medium for influencing people. It is a powerful tool if the optical and psychological aspects of color and form are employed to the greatest advantage," Mr. Cheskin continued.

GIVE YOUR PACKAGES "APPETITE APPEAL"

Attention vs. Holding Power

"Attracting attention and holding attention are two different and separate aspects of display. In considering attention power and holding power, we should know that of complementary colors, one has greater visibility and the other higher preference. One color has the power to attract and the other is pleasant to look at. One color very rarely has both attributes to any effective degree."

"The major colors and shapes in a display of packages, or any other display for marketing purposes, should be of high preference, to hold attention once the attention is there. However, there should also be a color or image, or both, with the primary purpose of attracting attention. If you have a display or package in several blue color values, you should have a spot of complementary yellow with which to attract attention. If the blues are soft and varied and of high preference, and the forms or images are also appealing, attention will be held after the yellow has attracted the eye. Likewise a magenta red display should have a brilliant green point of attraction. A predominantly green-blue or turquoise display should have an orange-red spot of attraction. In other words, the point of attraction is most effective when it is the exact complementary. Cool colors have high preference, but warm colors have greater visibility and attraction power." Mr. Cheskin pointed out the colors on a set of color charts and continued to explain.

Packaging Objective: to Inspire Action

"The final objective of a display of packages is, of course, to inspire action—to get the public to buy. Most purchases are emotionally inspired. Again we see the role of sensation transference. The display is unconsciously associated with the product itself. That is why a display with a combination of a visibility color, a number of colors of high preference, and shapes of high preference and easy retention in the memory is a most potent marketing tool."

"The tests with the detergent, margarine and gin, and many other such tests, show clearly that sensation transference is completely unconscious, that consumers have no idea color and design make them believe that one product is better than another. We cannot overemphasize the importance of sensation transference. There lies the secret of why a package with potent color and design brings increased sales."

"Sensation transference is the reason we judge a book by its cover, why we judge a man by the clothes he wears (and more consciously) a woman by the clothes she wears. Sensation transference is the reason an effective label sells canned goods and why an effectively designed bread wrapper sells bread. Bread is humble. It is simple. It is basic. It is an essential part of our daily diet. It is not glamorous nor stimulating, but like anything else basic, it can be successfully combined with glamorous, stimulating appetite appeal. Sensation transference will do the rest," Mr. Cheskin concluded.

We can give bread the appetite arousing association. We can show the bread in its glamorous surroundings. A classical author once said that surroundings are the difference between the prince and the pauper. We can give the stimulating, pleasure-producing surroundings to the humble and vital food—bread. We can do this on opaque waxed paper bread wrappers. Let the housewife be inspired by bread wrappers to serve bread attractively. We can have bread wrappers that promote both enjoyable and healthful eating.

A successful restaurant operator knows that people eat with their eyes. A good hostess serves food attractively to her guests because unconsciously, if not consciously, she knows people enjoy their food much more when it is attractively served. There are many essential foods that are not attractive. They lack eye appeal and even taste appeal. That is why they must be garnished.

Waxed paper has more than merely physical and practical advantages. We know that waxed paper is a most suitable packaging material, but brand and appetite imagery in correct colors that can be put on waxed paper are even more important than the physical and the practical aspects.

Effective brand identifying imagery combined with appetite appeal in high grade full color printing in-

spire interest in the consumer. They bring forth pleasant sensations, which through transference become
identified with your product, your brand, resulting in
favorable consumer attitudes toward your brand.

DOES COLOR GET THE CONSIDERATION IT DESERVES AS A MARKETING TOOL?

Tide—October 23, 1954

CHAPTER 13

Some marketers use color wisely and well in packaging, others lose business with the wrong hue.

ANY experienced marketer knows that a package is more than a container. Its size, shape, weight and composition—as well as its color—can be a strong influence on how well the product inside sells. On this last point, color as a marketing tool, many questions stand between the marketer and his sales goals.

To shed some light on these questions, Color Research Institute (Chicago) director, Louis Cheskin, came up last fortnight with a book that, at the very least, destroys some popular theories on color packaging and reinforces others popularly accepted. In his book, "Color Guide for Marketing Media," * Cheskin offers

* Color Guide for Marketing Media by Louis Cheskin (New York: The Macmillan Company, 1954).

some of his pointed opinions on the effective use of color as a marketing tool.

Cheskin at 46 has studied widely in art, psychology and Psychoanalysis. For twenty years or so, he has measured people's emotional reactions to color and design; for nine years (four as director) he has been associated with CRI. Says Cheskin: "The most important aspect of color (and imagery) as a marketing tool is preference. And preference is largely based on unconscious or subconscious associations." People, he adds, cannot tell what they like. For a number of psychological reasons they generally don't know what they like, and if they do think they know, they may not be willing to tell. To back up this theory, Cheskin cites some revealing case histories.

Besides his approach to color marketing, Cheskin takes a hearty whack at both the depth interview technique and esoteric designers.

The former, he charges, is not much more reliable than poll-taking since answers tend to vary with each interviewer, and since the respondent tends to philosophize, something she doesn't do in a supermarket. And as for esoteric designers, Cheskin believes much of their package design is ineffective because their sense of design is more highly developed than the consumer's and because they know little of physics, optics and psychology of color.

DOES COLOR GET CONSIDERATION?

Color Has Many Powers

A very important factor in merchandising, says Cheskin, is the power of color symbolism. There are numerous case histories of failures in export business because the exporter did not take into consideration the symbolic power of certain colors in the country to which the merchandise was being sent. Color symbolism, he explains, is not the same in all parts of the world. To Asiatics, for example, white, not black, symbolizes death and mourning.

While flippantly writing off the fact that "wrong symbolism can ruin a business and often does," Cheskin unfortunately supplies few examples of favorable instances—none where specific lessons can be learned from failures. However, the good examples, although perhaps rather obvious, are nonetheless interesting:

Procter & Gamble's Cheer has three billowing yellow, red and white images (associated with laundry) against the blue background (associated with cleanliness). These associations were revealed by extensive tests conducted on an unconscious level with consumers. In addition, other tests revealed highly favorable unconscious reactions to the images and colors. The package also rated high in the ocular tests.

Procter & Gamble's Crisco shortening label, because of favorable associations, was another example of an excellent marketing tool. Tests revealed that the label was associated with high quality. Favorable attitudes towards the oval and the colors were transferred to the product.

Lever Brothers' Good Luck margarine package reveals excellent image and color symbolism. The silver-foil package has a yellow circle and four-leaf clover on the front panel; the clover appears in smaller dimensions on the sides of the carton. The brand name is in the middle of the clover. Field tests conducted on an unconscious level with consumers revealed that both the yellow and the four-leaf clover have very favorable unconscious associations. The yellow, of course, symbolizes butter, which is desirable. The clover suggests good luck to the unconscious mind. This association is transferred to the product.

General Mills' Betty Crocker cake mix packages is a fine example of favorable symbolism. Consumer tests conducted on an unconscious level revealed that the red spoon (oval) produces very favorable reactions on an unconscious level. The particular Betty Crocker "red" is associated with kitchen and baking, but not with a living room. The results of the tests were confirmed by a tremendous increase in sales when the newly designed packages appeared on the market.

Such is the stuff the new Cheskin book is made of. It frankly is not the last word on enough important subjects relating to color. What it is, however, is a rather definitive treatise by Cheskin on the ins and outs of his CRI setup, interspersed with some fascinating sidelights on the wonderful world of color, and his ideas on harnessing its power to use as a means of influencing people. If you want to learn more about color—and you should—this is as good a place as any to begin.

PACKAGE APPRAISAL SANS
PERSONAL OPINION

Packaging Parade—August 1953

CHAPTER 14

ANNOUNCING its selection of the "Best Dressed Products of 1952," Color Research Institute, Chicago marketing research organization, recently named five products whose packages met selection requirements for the "best dressed" list. These packages are Procter & Gamble's Crisco; General Mills' Betty Crocker Cake Mix; Lever Brothers' Good Luck Margarine; Schulze & Burch's Flavor Kist Bleu Cheese Crackers; and Procter & Gamble's Cheer. Selection is based on a battery of optical and psychological tests, and the packages named are the only ones (of all those tested by the institute) passing all requirements.

Personal Opinions "Out"

Choice of packages for the "best dressed" list of products is based not on the opinions of any individuals or committee, but only on the results of the optical and psychological tests. Optical factors measured include visibility from a shelf, readability of a brand name, and eye-movement or attention-holding power of a package. Psychological factors measured involve the color and imagery of a package, as the tests determine color preference, color retention, and association of the color with the product or its use. Imagery is tested in the same manner as is color. Since the five above named packages rated highest with regard to these elements, the institute concludes that these packages are "outstanding," noting that every element of each package made a strong favorable impression. Louis Cheskin, director of the institute, pointed out that the testing program is based on getting the unconscious, unguarded reactions of consumers—not on their opinions or verbalisms. He asserted that those experienced with and conditioned to package design are even less able to express a reaction like that of a consumer. For example, ordinarily the institute tests contradict his own opinion. "However," he went on, "for the first time, my personal opinion and the test reports coincided, in the case of these five packages."

Nature of Tests

Optical tests utilize camera-type instruments, thus making possible the "pattern" type of ratings. As involved with these tests, visibility refers to the degree of visibility of a package, as displayed on store shelves. Readability refers to the degree of readability of the brand name on a package. Eye-movement, or attention-holding power, determines: Do the eyes travel smoothly over the entire package or does the package design cause eye fatigue? Does the package get and hold attention? The eye-movement test is an optical measurement for evaluating the package as a whole. Most of the psychological tests deal with parts or components of packages. These involve statistical ratings, determining matters of color and imagery. The tests in regard to color determine what percentage of consumers likes the colors on a package, what percentage of them remembers the colors, and what percentage of them associates the colors with the product or brand.

Similarly, regarding imagery, the tests determine percentages of consumers who like the image or trademark, who remember it, and who associate it with the product or the use of the product. All of these tests are conducted on an unconscious level, meaning that the consumer does not know what is actually being tested or determined.

Unconscious Level

These tests must be conducted on an unconscious level because, in a store or market, a consumer is rarely conscious of color and design as such, the institute explained. Thus a shopper is not aware that colors and design influence selection of a product. In making tests, it is necessary to have a similar kind of psychological testing condition, in order to determine unconscious

preferences. "Remember that there is a difference between a consumer's stated opinion and her actual, unconscious preference," Mr. Cheskin warned, noting
that preference involves self-interest, in making a
choice, while opinion does not. Preference means that
the consumer actually wants the article, while her opinion does not necessarily mean that she wants it. Also,
one stating an opinion often expresses what he or she
believes the listener wants to hear. Thus, the institute
does not interview, because too much depends on the
skill of the interviewer, and does not poll, because
people's opinions are not the same as their actual preferences. Further, verbalisms which people express are
not the same as their actual behavior patterns. Above
all, the consumer must not know what is being tested.

Consumer Opinions Valueless

The institute objects, for example, to asking a panel
of women to decide which design they prefer for a given
package. Reasons for this objection are (1) it makes
them conscious of package design, while in actual practice they do not realize how package design influences
their choice of product or brand; (2) it makes art critics
out of them; (3) it places the package design in the cate-
gory of fashion and decoration, and (4) no self-interest
is involved in expressing an opinion. "Remember,"
Mr. Cheskin observed, "simply because a woman says
she likes something does not mean she will buy it."
Another serious problem in regard to opinions is that

typical consumers cannot tell one how they think, how they react, or how they feel about a product. The institute cited a case where three packages, each containing exactly the same coffee, were presented to housewives. The container of one of these was of a special type. Some 82 per cent of these women, when queried, said they did not care what kind of container they got, as long as they got the same kind of coffee that was in the special container. Only 4 per cent consciously wanted the special container, as such. Thus, the 82 per cent group was not aware that the package conditioned its attitude toward the coffee; as noted, the coffee in all packages was exactly the same.

Details of Testing

In getting accurate reactions from consumers, the institute uses such tests as those of the free-association type. For example, a test of a bread wrapper revolves around a home situation. The furnishings, hygienic factors, or food preparation are involved. Individuals being tested do not know that the wrapper is the object of the test. Thus, their associations, reactions are candid, unguarded, and are given at the unconscious level.

The institute does not test the package as a whole only; also tested are parts of the package—such as the colors and the figure or design on the front—to get accurate, specific results. There are important reasons for not testing only all of the package, the institute asserts. Finding out that one package is better than another does not tell that the better is the best possible marketing tool.

Finding that a package in general is a poor marketing tool does not reveal that package's specific weaknesses. Instead, by testing components, one learns whether a specific element is strong or weak. Then, it becomes possible to make specific changes to correct what is found weak.

Designers of the "Winners"

Of these "best dressed" products, two of these five packages were designed by Donald Deskey Associates of New York City. These two are the new Crisco package and the Cheer package, both of which are products of Procter & Gamble. Edward Gustave Jacobsson, of New York City, designed the Good Luck margarine package, which is a product of Lever Brothers. Charles E. Akers, Chicago designer, developed the Flavor-Kist Bleu Cheese Crackers package for that product's manufacturer, Schulze & Burch Biscuit Company. The design of the Betty Crocker packages was the teamwork effort of a group of designers associated with Batten, Barton, Durstine & Osborn, Inc., advertising agency serving General Mills, producer of the Betty Crocker line. The final cake mix packages were designed by Lippincott and Margulies.

ARE "WRONG" COLORS WRECKING YOUR PACKAGE?

Food Marketing Magazine—October 1953

CHAPTER 15

TODAY'S package can no longer be a mere container with a picture on it. If it is to be an effective marketing tool, it must be engineered, functionally designed, and imbued with psychological power.

A merchandising manager recently asked, "Do you advise that we get the services of a top-notch designer to produce a half dozen package designs and then ask a panel of consumers which of the six designs they like best?"

Getting a top-notch designer, I recommend very strongly, but at Color Research Institute we do not recommend asking consumers to judge packages. Consumers cannot tell what they like, or why they like anything, or what they will do about the package when they get to the store. This is demonstrated very clearly by the following case history.

"WRONG" COLORS

Attracted by Special Container

Three packages of instant coffee were presented to
housewives. Three weeks later, a researcher asked them
which of the three they preferred and told them that
the manufacturer would present them with a half dozen
packages of their preferred blend. 86 per cent replied
that they preferred the coffee that had come in a specially designed container.

Then the researcher asked each housewife whether
she would object if the same coffee were sent to her in
one of the other two kinds of containers (a stock glass
jar or a can). Eighty-two per cent said they did not care
in what kind of container the coffee came as long as it
was the same blend as in the special container; 4 per
cent of the homemakers said they wanted the coffee in
the special container.

This test showed that 4 per cent of the consumers
were conscious of the container, whereas 82 per cent
were not aware that the package conditioned their attitudes to the coffee. All three packages—the specially
designed one, the jar, and the can—contained the same
blend of coffee.

A large majority of the consumers had transferred
the sensation from the package to the product.

Unconscious Influence

In the market place, each stack of packages produces
a pattern of color and image sensations that have a

strong influence on the shopper, nearly always on an unconscious level. Rarely is a consumer aware that she is influenced by the color and design of a package.

That is why reliable marketing research is based on consumers' unconscious, uninhibited, unguarded reactions, not on opinions or verbalisms.

At Color Research Institute all tests are either association tests conducted on an unconscious level or preference tests conducted by an indirect method. The association tests are devised so that the consumers do not know what is being tested. In the preference test, self-interest is always involved.

Of course, packages must be designed before they can be tested. Designers follow certain fundamental principles in creating packages; through experience they have learned to employ various eye-catching devices. An experienced designer has considerable skill in manipulating images and patterns. But even some of the best practitioners have little knowledge about the effect various colors have on the great body of consumers or shoppers.

Three Reasons for Failure

There are at least three reasons why many package designs are not effective marketing tools.

First: A top-notch designer is generally a highly educated individual with a highly developed color sense, which is not at all characteristic of the typical or average consumer.

Second: Some designers have had considerable training in graphic arts but have had little training in color.

Third, and most important: Until recent years, there has been little scientific knowledge about color. Only in the last decade has there been any serious attempt to study the optical and psychological aspects of color.

The following are a few outstanding facts we have recently learned about the nature of color.

Of greatest value is the knowledge that colors should be used in complementary pairs, because the relationship between complementary colors is physical, physiological, and psychological. Complementary hues comprise the total visible spectrum, are physiological pairs in the eyes, and provide a psychological balance of warmth and coolness. In other words, complementary colors are physically, optically, and also psychologically balanced.

The easiest way to understand the nature of color is to recognize that every hue has a mate and a family. The complementary hue is the mate and the related values—shades, tints, and tones—are the family.

Complementary Colors Preferred

According to traditional aesthetic concepts, use of complementary colors is in good taste. Actually, acquired taste has little to do with this preference, since, for physical and optical reasons, it is as natural for normal people to like complementary colors as it is for them to walk upright.

Where complementary color combinations are not preferred, there is likely to be some kind of special conditioning or an adverse economic factor. This is indicated by the fact that many primitive people create designs in complementary colors, whereas discordant color conglomerations are often found in industrial slums.

Preference tests made by an indirect method at Color Research Institute to probe unconscious levels suggest that colors normally affect people in accordance with specific laws. Some colors have high preference ratings, others extremely low ones.

It was found that some colors rate higher with men than with women and vice versa (men usually preferring deep shades while women like delicate tints), and that some hues get progressively higher or lower preference ratings as they are diluted or neutralized with increasing amounts of white or gray.

The preference rating of a color is conditioned not only by its specific value but also by the presence of other colors, by the area it occupies, and by the object with which it is associated.

Green and Red Go Well

When a color is used with its complementary, the preference rating usually rises. Thus, green has increased appeal when it is used near magenta red, and orange-red becomes more acceptable in the company of green-blue. Presumably, of course, this is due to the physical and optical relationship between complementary colors. However, a warm red which may be pleasing against a neutral background sometimes is found much too vibrant when associated with its complementary green, particularly if the green is not sufficiently diluted or neutralized. The same is true about other complementaries.

Kitchen Colors

Associations, or symbolic elements, strongly affect color preference ratings. For example, magenta red, which has a high general preference rating, drops in rating when it is put into the kitchen. Orange-red, which has one of the lowest general preference ratings, increases in preference when used in the kitchen. Colors of the peach-pink group receive increased preference ratings when associated with cosmetics and drop in preference when linked with hardware.

A large percentage of people show preference for a certain green when that color is associated with a vacation. The same green drops in preference when it is used with various food products. Another green has a high rating when associated with food but a low rating when associated with clothing.

Rarity is also a factor in color preference. Colors seen only occasionally possess the emotionally stimulating elements of surprise and newness. Common colors, like common foods, are monotonous; they may become tiresome, boring and thus prompt us to look for new color sensations.

Another fact about color preference is that it does not necessarily coincide with color retention. Yellow, for instance, has a low preference rating but a high retention rating. In other words, although yellow is not well liked it is easily recalled. Peach, on the other hand, while a favorite with most people, is difficult to remember. Some colors, however, have the same ratings for preference and for retention.

Tests conducted at Color Research Institute on the basis of what people want (not what they say they like) also reveal that there are geographic, national, cultural, and economic factors in color preference. For example, a specific red received a much higher preference rating with Italians and Mexicans than with Scandinavians and New Englanders. And it had a much higher preference rating with Italians in low-income groups than with upper middle class Italians.

Delicate Shades Attract Wealthy People

A cool magenta red had a very high general preference rating but a much lower one among the underprivileged. A grass-green color had a low preference rating in rural communities and a very high rating in a steel mill community. Higher education and higher income coincided with preference for delicate colors. Illiteracy and poverty coincided with preference for brilliant colors.

"WRONG" COLORS

For practical purposes, research showed that persons who had many emotional outlets through culture and/or ability to purchase emotional satisfaction showed a preference for diluted and neutralized colors.

Those who had opportunity for only limited emotional outlets (either because of lack of education or because of low income) showed a distinct preference for pure hues in large doses, particularly for those that were warm, such as orange-red and orange. In the slums, the nearer the colors are to the rainbow the more enticing they are.

Blue-Green Tops Yellow-Green

Generally speaking, magenta red and blue are very popular colors, but yellow-green has a low preference rating. A blue-green has much higher preference than a yellow-green.

Although popular as a pure hue, magenta red becomes generally unacceptable when diluted with white. A pure orange-red has a very low preference rating, but when mixed with white, and thus converted into peach, its preference rating is high.

We should always remember that color is hardly ever isolated from imagery or pattern, and by its nature color occupies area or space. All of the related factors have an influence on color preference.

Colors have varying degrees of appeal, diverse favorable or unfavorable associations, and different degrees

177

of retention in the memory. Colors are also factors in visibility and in legibility. Having a package with maximum effectiveness as a marketing tool means making use of the recent scientific findings about the nature of color.

COLOR PLAYS AN IMPORTANT ROLE

Retail Advertising Week—April 5, 1948

CHAPTER 16

IF WE consider only our conscious reactions, the role of color seems to be a superficial one. However, we must realize that only a fraction of our actions and reactions is conscious and that most of our feelings or sensations remain unconscious and never reach the point of becoming complete conceptions or even significant perceptions. Therefore, in order to grasp the full meaning of the effects that colors have on people's emotions, we must deal with the unconscious and not with the conscious aspects of color.

Scientifically conducted tests have shown that spectrum hues have a physical, physiological and psychological relationship. We have learned that color harmony is not an acquired "sense of taste" or a development of an "aesthetic sense" but is a physical phenomenon. In order to use color effectively we should be aware that color harmony is basically physical and at the same time optical. Actually, color is a manifestation of the relationship between matter and light (energy) as is demonstrated by the fact that the primary components of light are the exact complements to the primary components of pigment (matter). Color harmony is physiological in that we have eyes that can receive color waves. Many animals, among them dogs, cats, horses and cows, cannot see colors.

Testing under controlled conditions has demonstrated that hues have specific psychological effects on human beings. For example, colors of the red family produce sensations of warmth, whereas colors of the blue family create sensations of coolness. However, we must keep in mind that the warmth and coolness are optical sensations and psychological effects, not thermostatic measurements.

We should be aware that the value (intensity, lightness or darkness) of a color is also an optical factor and has a psychological effect. Color value is optical because it affects our vision in the amount of white light it reflects. It is psychological because it creates moods. Thus, the value of a color is a determining factor whether it has a favorable or unfavorable effect.

Color acts on emotion, not on reason. You can often change a person's ideas but not his emotional responses. People are not emotionally "set" about most objects or merchandise in general, but reactions to colors and to some images are established in early life.

The cultural and educational background of the consumer must always be given consideration because culture and education have a great influence on color preference. Economic status is another vital factor in color appeal.

COLOR PLAYS AN IMPORTANT ROLE

Since color effectiveness differs with various social groups, an advertisement selling a 10-cent article requires colors radically different from one selling a $100 article.

The right color possesses the following attributes:

1. It has a specific psychological effect. It produces a definite emotional response. It is stimulating or calming, soothing or irritating.
2. It has symbolic meaning. Some colors symbolize delicacy, others denote strength. There are colors for expressing dignity and colors that symbolize quality. Some colors indicate danger and some indicate safety.
3. It attracts or holds attention. Some colors attract the eye and get attention. Other colors hold the attention.
4. It has specific identity and retention power. Some colors are remembered more easily than other colors or black and white. Brand identity can be built with an appropriate color. Some brands should be identified by a high preference color, some by a color that rates high in memory retention or recall.

Making effective use of color power means choosing the appropriate color for the purpose. It means considering color in the light of preference, association and retention ratings.

The following three factors, among others, should be determined in the analysis of a color in relation to a specific problem: (1) the psychological effect of the specific color on the social group it will reach, (2) the symbolic relationship of the color to the product, (3) the attention getting power and retention power of the specific hue, shade or tint.

The eye-movement or eye-flow of the layout is very important. In evaluating the effectiveness of an ad, or point-of-sale poster, the following conditions must first be established: (1) what the nature of the product is, (2) whom it is intended to serve, (3) when it will be presented, (4) where it will appear.

The layout should always express the character of the product. The social and economic status of those whom the advertisement is to reach must at all times be considered. The time of year and the general economic and social conditions should not be overlooked. The kind of publication in which the advertisement is to appear is also an important factor.

Research has shown that we should never consider color as a separate element, independent of form or imagery. Color and imagery are interdependent.

The Color Research Institute has developed a scientific procedure for determining the effectiveness of an ad or other sales tool before it is put before the public. Advertising matter is now tested before it is published or released. Tests are used to determine:

1. The preference rating of the image.
2. The retention rating of the image.
3. The symbolism rating of the image.

4. The preference rating of the color.
5. The retention rating of the color.
6. The symbolism rating of the color.
7. Visibility of the layout.
8. Legibility of the copy.
9. How the eyes travel over the layout.

The first six tests are psychological and statistical. If 85 out of 100 individuals react favorably to an image, it gets a preference rating of 85. If 80 out of 100 individuals recall the image, it receives a retention rating of 80. Colors are rated in the same manner.

The symbolism rating is important because association of the color or image with a product is an important factor in merchandising. As stated before, images and colors can be used to symbolize the product or brand. Some images and colors can be used to symbolize the quality or character of the product. A circle may symbolize the world, a triangle may symbolize strength. Certain reds symbolize danger, some blues symbolize distance. Some symbols reach the conscious mind, some have an effect on the unconscious mind.

The last three tests—visibility, legibility, and eye-movement—are instrument measurements determining optical effectiveness.

An analysis is made on the basis of all nine ratings. This scientific approach to advertising is the best assurance of having an effective ad campaign.

A PRIMER FOR SELECTING COLORS
WITH SALES APPEAL

Sales Management—June 15, 1948

CHAPTER 17

Based on an interview with Louis Cheskin, Associate Director, Color Research Institute.

Why do certain colors exert an almost magnetic pull on buyers? How do color preferences vary from area-to-area and among races? Can you pre-test package colors? Mr. Cheskin gives a quick review of how and why people react.

BROWN can help you sell coffee, Boston baked beans or tobacco. It is effective in labeling and packaging. Blue, properly used, can be an important aid in merchandising hardware items. Pink can move cosmetics from the shelves of the dealer. Some greens are first-class colors for a jeweler to use, for somehow, they seem to be associated with precious things.

If you want to sell books or magazines by mail, then go the whole hog and let your printed matter carry red, blue, yellow—but in the right values and proportions so that one color will provide the needed visibility, another the necessary readability, and all of them a favorable psychological effect.

The above paragraphs work all right for an opening statement. Get into the subject, however, and shortly you will find that there's a lot more to it than that. For one thing, there are hundreds of hues, thousands of shades, tones and tints, and a person may react differently to two tints of the same hue though they may seem to be almost alike.

"We have been doing research for several years in an effort to find out what colors make the cash register ring," says Louis Cheskin, associate director in charge of test production at Color Research Institute laboratories in Chicago. He is also author of the book, published last year, titled, "Colors—What They Can Do For You." Until recently the institute has hoarded its findings vigilantly, considering its information valuable private property, but now it is ready to let many of its discoveries be known.

In all this research, aimed to find out why a buyer will pick up one can or package or product and let others remain on the shelves, much more than color alone was put under the microscope. Before the research work had been carried far it became certain that the job was filled with traps, pits and ambushes, some of them so tricky that they are likely, unless caught, to lead the whole study up a blind alley. Here is a sample of how this can work:

Eighty-five women were shown a display of six babushkas. They were asked: "Which of them do you consider the most beautiful?"

Sixty-eight of the women chose the same pattern. Then, after their minds had been diverted from the subject, each woman was told to take a babushka as a reward. Of the 68 women only nine selected the design they had picked as the most beautiful.

Eye Appeal

Display the same product in identical cans or packages, but with different labels and ask any group of people, "Which is the handsomest label?" and you will invariably get the same answer from all of them, says Mr. Cheskin. To the last man or woman they will pick the one with the most colors and the most intricate artwork. Five or six colors on the label always get them.

Invite them to pick up a can and take it home and you are certain to get a different answer. Your guinea pig will almost always choose a plain label of not more than two colors carrying lettering that is easily read and with no gingerbread artwork at all.

Human nature is such that if you let a subject know why he is being tested his answer is likely to be thrown off. The babushka women above, for example, thought they were being asked to select the most beautiful. They chose a colorful and intricate design. They gave the manufacturer his answer, however, when they unconsciously picked the one they would most desire to possess. He was interested only in which number a woman would be most likely to buy.

The reason that a brown label on a can will sell coffee better than violet, green, blue or orange label is what is called "association of ideas." Not any hit-or-miss brown will do. The shade of brown must be carefully and scientifically selected. Get just the right value and, associating the label with the rich, brown coffee bean, the buyer will almost smell the aroma of the fresh coffee and taste its goodness. Subconsciously he will pick up that can.

Beans and Hardware

The next time you go shopping in a grocery store look over the display of baked beans in tins. Note how you are "stopped" by Libby's Deep-Brown Beans. The label is preponderantly a crusty, tasty brown with just a touch of red and yellow. Unconsciously you are likely to reach for this can. The label makes you sense the taste and aroma of its contents because our senses co-operate in bringing a sense of pleasure.

Blue, with a little red on it, has been proved an excellent color for use in building sales in the hardware trade. Used in direct-mail literature, in labels or in point-of-sale signs, the Color Research Institute has proved that it will do a far better than average job. There must be a reason for this and the researchers think they have the answer.

Color Association

Subconsciously we are all likely to think of fine tools as being made of live, blue, vibrant steel. In advertising we read about blue razor blades. Blue blades, we are told, are made of a sort of super-steel. Much steel, of course, is not blue at all, but unconsciously, somehow, we feel that it is. And, so, all fine metal objects become more or less blue in our subconscious minds.

Red is a strong color. We associate it with virility and power. Blue blades of battle and the red of blood go together. We associate them in our inner minds so they become complementary, and together they sell hardware.

"There are not nearly so many Yellow Cabs on the street as you think there are," says the color-conscious Mr. Cheskin. "They hit you hard in the eye because they have a high rating in what we call 'retention value.' There are colors that we like and colors that we dislike. Certain colors, and I am speaking of the hundreds recognized on our color charts, will soothe and calm you. Others may be disturbing. They may even affect one violently. Some persons have such utter dislikes for certain colors that they will almost cause them to gag."

What Determines Tastes?

The likes and dislikes for colors can be geographical, racial or they may be governed by sex. Social and financial backgrounds, tests have shown, are certain to affect them. Different colors appeal, speaking from the viewpoint of the mass, to people who live on our gold coasts, back of the yards, or in rural sections.

Green labels and packages will not have much influence in getting a farmer or his wife to buy your goods. They see so much green . . . the grassy pastures, the wheat, the oats, the corn and all growing things . . . that green hardly registers with them. Probably they all love green. Intimate to them that green leaves them cold and they will be the first to deny it. The answer of the research men to all this is merely that green does not sell farm people.

The Scandinavian is fond of bright blues and greens as a rule; the Italian has a preference for warm reds; dark brown will repel the Negro but yellow will attract him; Mrs. Gotrocks, the chances are, will fall for magenta; Mrs. Schmalz, who lives in a blighted area, will go for bright green because she sees so little of it. Toss a batch of toys to a group of pre-kindergarten children of the rich and the little dears will go into battle for the red ones, just as will all other normal kids. The children living in slums, where they see little green, will settle for green toys as second choice.

"Experts" Disagree

Artists and businessmen, and even advertising experts, all too often know little about "selling" colors, Mr. Cheskin has found. He tells a story of twelve package designs which were shown to various specialists and experts for their judgment. This is what happened:

No. 7 Was picked as best by a jury of artists.
No. 11 Was picked as best by a group of agency executives.
No. 12 Was picked as best by the manufacturer for whom it was designed.

When this impasse was reached the proposition was put up to a considerable number of prospective buyers of the product. To the surprise of everyone, 86 per cent of them chose No. 4, which up to that time had been a sleeper. And remember, the market research man will tell anyone at the drop of the hat, the trick is to find out what the buyer will buy, not what he thinks he likes.

That there are "shade preferences" within a color was amply proved not long ago, when a manufacturer made up six packages. They were alike in dimensions text, surface design—and all were red. There was one difference. Each package was a different shade of red. When a test was made among purchasers, 76 per cent of them selected one particular shade.

Color for Emphasis

Color can become a convenience factor. Example: A toothpaste tube had a white cap. When the cap was laid on the white top of a wash basin the user generally had some difficulty finding it. This created irritation.

When the cap was changed to red it reduced annoyance and the product picked up in sales.

A candy manufacturer packed a $3 box of candy in a container that cost him 14 cents, but he put a $1.50 box in a 30-cent container. His reasoning was simple. Those who bought the $3 box of candy threw the container away as soon as it was empty. Those who received the $1.50 package were likely to keep the box and treasure it, using it for many purposes for a long time.

His theory was that the person who would plunk down $3 for a box of candy was buying candy. The poorer person, usually a young fellow buying a gift for his girl, was buying candy plus the container. He was really giving her two gifts in one. Also, people with low incomes can't afford to buy appropriate containers for buttons, small change and costume jewelry.

Two toothbrushes sold side by side in many drug stores are another example of how the package figures in the sale. One brush, priced at 50 cents, is packaged in a two-color container printed in cool, delicate shades. The other, which sells for 30 cents, is contained in a three-color box printed in hot vivid colors. Each package appeals to its own group of buyers.

Two packages of a cosmetic were placed on sale side by side. Content and packages were alike except that one package was pink while the other was yellow. Ninety-six out of the first 100 women who made a purchase picked the pink package. When another cosmetic house changed a package from blue to peach sales immediately tripled.

Research has brought to light a number of facts which are important in building window or other displays. Black, for instance, is not effective for window backgrounds. It is depressing, it lacks attraction power, it absorbs a great deal of light. It can be used to advantage, however, if very little black is shown and if the articles displayed are brilliantly colored. Black articles, and white as well, should be shown against a background of delicate cool color. The best of these are blue-green, green-blue or violet-blue. Gray, a neutral color, has little effect upon adjacent items.

Color Ads Boost Sales

The color research carried on by the Color Research Institute has developed other important sales data. A mail order house, for example, printed half of its catalog in black-and-white; in the other half it used color for illustrations. The color pages pulled fifteen times better than the black and white.

A stove manufacturer who had been using black-and-white turned to color and his returns were 395 per cent greater. A clothing manufacturer got 338 inquiries from a black-and-white advertisement in a magazine. When he ran the same advertisement in color in the same magazine he received 1,334 inquiries.

A paint company for one of its mailings used blue letterheads and yellow envelopes. Then it reversed the mailing, using yellow letterheads and blue envelopes. The blue letterhead in the yellow envelope outpulled the yellow letterhead in the blue envelope by 450 per cent!

There is a scientific explanation for this. Yellow, according to the findings of the institute, has the highest "retention value" of all colors. That means that it hits you harder in the eye and you will remember it longer. But it doesn't make the customer buy because it has a low preference rating.

COLOR EFFECTIVENESS CAN
BE MEASURED

The American Printer—July 1948

CHAPTER 18

Traditional concepts of color were proved wrong
when the Color Research Institute tested people's
wants and not expressed likes. Color preference,
image preference, and retention power of designs,
altogether, are determining factors in advertising
effectiveness.

MERCHANDISING and advertising specialists are
aware that color somehow increases results. They use
such words as "distinctive," "attractive," "natural," in
describing their choice. However, many color users
still have no way of knowing, except through trial and
error, which color or combination of colors will be
most effective for a particular purpose. Most executives
and specialists feel their way. They are guided by their
best judgment; fundamentally, personal taste prevails.

Very often an advertising or merchandising specialist
changes a design or color merely to "get something
new." Since he has no factual information as to public

preference the change has to be based on personal judgment. Yet a new color scheme will not necessarily appeal to the general public any more than the old one, nor is his favorite color necessarily the favorite color of the people the advertising piece is to reach. The fact that he is tired of the same old color or colors does not mean that the public is. Therefore, although it may be advisable to strike a new note with a new advertisement, a new color scheme in the product or on the package can often result in disaster.

Color preference is a deep seated element of people's character. It is usually ingrained in the individual's unconscious mind. Color works on emotion, not on reason, and, although you can often change a person's ideas, it is almost impossible to alter his emotional responses.

For greatest effectiveness in packaging, or in advertising, colors as well as images must be chosen objectively by scientific methods. Tests have proved that the merchandiser's choice is not between black-and-white and color but between using mere colors and using colors that have the most favorable effect.

Image and Color Preferences Are Rated

At the Color Research Institute, we do not approach marketing research by testing preferences of package designs or magazine advertisements, or direct mail literature. We first determine the preference ratings of the images and the colors.

Everything in life consists of images and colors. We naturally describe all things by image and color. We say "a short man in a blue suit," "a tall girl in a beige dress," "a large blue chair."

All visual sensations produced by inanimate objects are both sensations of imagery and sensations of color. We want to learn, therefore, which types of images produce favorable sensations and which unfavorable, and which types of colors produce favorable sensations and which unfavorable ones.

The Color Research Institute did not undertake to test design preference until it had the necessary information about the elements that make up a package design.

Our first project was to acquire preference ratings of 120 colors (thirty hues, thirty shades, thirty tints, and thirty tones). We later tested 680 colors (the Ostwald System) and later we developed our own color system of 960 colors, 480 of which were given preference tests.

We did not continue with our color preference tests because we soon learned that colors normally affect people in accordance with specific natural laws.

We found, for example, that some hues rate higher with men than with women, or vice versa, and that some hues get progressively higher preference ratings, and others progressively lower ratings, when they are diluted with increasing amounts of white or neutralized with increasing amounts of gray.

The most important part of the new information was the correlation between diluting hues with white (or neutralizing with gray) and color preference. The fact that there is coordination between physical color mixtures and optical-psychological effects was a most astonishing discovery.

(Note that I describe color mixing as a physical process, not chemical. Color mixing is chemical in nature only when the chemicals are of different and non-assimilating chemical origin, such as mixing a sulphur color with a lead or copper color. Mixing colors that have chemical affinity is a physical process because adding a color means subtracting an additional portion from the light.)

Color and Psychology

Most people consider color preference a purely subjective matter. Obviously, color preference is not merely a subjective matter when we know that there is a correlation between degrees of color preference and degrees of hue modification.

We learned something that was still more devastating to our traditional concepts about color. We found by using psychoanalytic techniques that persons who show abnormal color preference also possess other characteristics that are different from the normal.

And we learned that strong color phobias and abnormal reactions to certain colors could be traced to traumatic experiences of early childhood.

Individuals who hated red could, through a psychoanalytic process, trace the feeling to a very unpleasant childhood experience with red. Persons who despised blue could trace it back to a similar association in early childhood.

Also, women who had a preference for colors normally preferred by men showed other masculine characteristics. Men who had a preference for delicate tints showed other effeminate traits.

Some colors had the same preference ratings with men and with women, and again, in keeping with specific laws, these are the neutral color values. Color in this way demonstrates what practicing psychologists have always contended—men have a little of the feminine in them and women have a little of the masculine.

Physically neutral colors are psychologically neutral. They are not offensive to men and they are not offensive to women. Neither do they call forth strong emotional responses from either men or women.

We also learned that the six hues of the visible spectrum produce specific emotions that do not vary in degree but have either a negative or positive effect, whereas other hues and color values (tints, tones, and shades) produce reactions in various degrees of intensity or depth.

For example, a person does not (consciously or unconsciously) like pure violet-blue very much, pure green-blue a little less, and pure green still less. He either likes the pure color or he does not like it. The reaction is not a matter of degree but is merely negative or positive, unfavorable or favorable.

With the color values, however, such as dark blue,

lighter blue, and very light blue, there are degrees of preference. A person will like the dark blue the best, the lighter blue a little less, and the lightest blue still less, but he still reacts favorably to all blues. It can be just the opposite, where the individual reacts most favorably to the very lightest blue, a little less favorably to the darker blue and still less favorably to the very dark blue. Making a hue a little more greenish or slightly more bluish will also lower or increase the preference.

Again our traditional concepts of color have been proved wrong. We generally do not differentiate between the numerous pure hues and tonal color values and the spectrum hues. Now we learn that there is a sharp separation between some of the hues, the spectrum hues creating strong negative or positive sensations, and that other hues and color values produce sensations in depth, that is, various degrees of sensations and responses.

How did we conduct the tests? First we did what everyone else did. We asked hundreds of people which of thirty hues they liked best and which of the tints, tones, and shades. We developed some pretty fancy charts on color preferences and we were primarily concerned with types of samplings, with social strata.

Then one day we found we had some colored paper and a number of pictures to dispose of because we were liquidating a project. I decided that some of the material should be used as a medium for conducting a test, with the surplus going as prizes.

Then we learned something shocking. The colored papers and the pictures judged to be the most beautiful remained on the shelves, while papers and pictures the audience judged to be poor were taken home as prizes.

This test caused us to re-examine all our tests. We began to conduct tests on the basis of what people wanted instead of on what they said was beautiful. We found then that the results from the two types of tests differed greatly. In other words, we learned that people's expressed likes do not coincide with their actual wants.

All of our beautiful tabulations and charts had to be discarded and we began to conduct tests on the basis of people's wants. That is when we learned that physical gradation of colors corresponded with preference gradation and that normal color preference is based on specific laws.

The tests on the basis of what people want also reveal that in addition to the inherent basic color preference, there are geographic, national, and cultural differences and that economic status is a factor in color preference.

For example, we found that a specific orange-red had a very low rating with all groups of people, but that it had a much higher rating with Italians and Mexicans than it did with those of Scandinavian origin or with New England backgrounds. And it had a much higher rating with Italians of a low income group than with upper middle class Italians.

COLOR EFFECTIVENESS CAN BE MEASURED

A cool magenta red we found had a very high preference rating but it had a much lower preference
among the underprivileged than it did among the upper
middle classes. A grass green color had a low preference
rating in rural communities and a very high preference rating in a steel mill community.

We found that the geographic factors were most decisive in the pure hues whereas the cultural and economic factors were most decisive in color values (tints
and tones). For example, Scandinavians preferred certain blues, Slavs preferred certain reds, and Latins
other reds, but it made little difference whether the
blues were delicate or strong or whether the reds
were diluted or pure.

Higher education and higher income coincided with
preference for delicate colors. Illiteracy and poverty
coincided with preferences for brilliant colors.

We tried samplings of newly rich persons with little
education and individuals with much education, but
with low income. The results were most interesting
though not conclusive, since the samplings were too
small. The two groups had the same color preferences
and they were only slightly different from the general
upper middle class. For practical purposes the research
showed that those people who had many emotional
outlets through culture and/or the ability to purchase
emotional satisfaction showed a preference for diluted
and neutralized hues. Those who had the opportunity
only for limited emotional outlets (either because of
lack of education or because of inability to purchase

them in the form of amusements) showed a distinct preference for pure hues. For the underprivileged, the nearer the colors were to the rainbow the better.

Men Prefer Angles

At this point, we had considerable knowledge about the nature of color but, before we could go into measuring packaging and advertising effectiveness, we had to learn the nature of images.

We employed numerous images, such as ovals, triangles, rectangles, scrolls, brunettes, blondes, red heads, young men, old men, Indians, cowboys, and we set out to learn which of these images people like the best. We received some very enlightening information.

We found that women like curves and men prefer angles (and I was of the belief until then that men prefer curves). And we learned that certain shapes have much greater preference ratings than others. We learned, for example, that an oval has greater preference with both men and women than an octagon.

At this point we had an additional guide for marketing research but we soon realized that color preference and image preference are only two factors in building product identity and in creating sales. We learned that although a color has a high preference rating it may have very low retention power, that is, it is difficult to recall.

Our next step was to take the colors and the images and test them for retention and we received this type of information: that yellow has a very low preference rating but a very high retention rating; that peach has a high preference rating but a low retention rating.

Of the images, we found out that the simpler the image the higher the retention rating but, like color, a high image retention rating did not necessarily mean a high preference rating. However, we did learn that certain colors and certain images have about the same retention and preference ratings.

We now had preference and retention ratings for colors and preference and retention ratings for images. But this information still was not a yardstick for measuring package design or advertising effectiveness because we found that the association factor was still another element that had a strong effect on preference and retention.

We found out that there are certain colors with strong symbolic meanings that modify color preference radically. For example, we learned that a certain magenta red, with a very high preference rating, fell to a low rating as soon as it was put into the kitchen. And orange-red that has a very low preference rating increased in preference when associated with kitchen stool seat covers, walls and utensils.

All types of symbolism were devastating to color preference ratings. For example, colors of the peach-pink family received slightly increased preference ratings when associated with cosmetics and dropped to the bottom when associated with hardware.

Colors of the blue family dropped greatly when associated with cosmetics but increased in association with hardware. A specific green was high in preference rating when associated with a vacation and it dropped in rating when associated with a food product. Another green had a high preference rating when associated with jewelry but fell when associated with cosmetics.

We began to test image symbolism and found that image ratings were also modified by specific associations but not to the same extent as colors.

It became evident that both images and colors required symbolism ratings based on what is known in psychology as free association tests. We also conducted some research on traditional color and image symbolism in various countries, an important factor in export business.

Six Ratings

We could now take a package or a design and evaluate it from six aspects:

1. An image preference rating.
2. An image retention rating.
3. A color preference rating.
4. A color retention rating.
5. An image symbolism rating.
6. A color symbolism rating.

We began rating the dominant color or colors of the packages on the basis of accumulated data in our files. We did the same with images. Although now we rarely get a design with a color for which we do not have a rated swatch, we do get images for which we have no ratings. In these cases we conduct preference, retention and association tests with the specific image.

When a package or label design receives the six ratings listed above we have considerable knowledge about the nature of the design but we still don't know how it rates in competition with other packages. Suppose a package scores high in all six ratings. The high ratings would still be useless unless the package is seen by the shoppers.

There are colors that have high preference and retention ratings and these may also have high symbolism ratings but still have very poor visibility.

We found that the human eye cannot judge the visibility of a package. Tests have shown that in a group of ten persons there are about five concepts of visibility. We therefore developed an optical instrument for measuring visibility from the shelf.

We know that the product name and other important information should have the best possible readability. The lettering or type faces are therefore measured for their readability by similar instruments.

Now we are ready to determine how the various elements relate to each other. After we know we have images and colors with the highest possible ratings and have achieved the highest possible visibility and best possible readability, we are ready to evaluate the design as a whole.

Here again we do not depend on personal judgment

to tell us whether the design (or layout) is well composed. The design (or layout) gets an eye-movement test that shows whether the eyes move smoothly over the unit, or whether an important part, image or copy, is skipped or causes hesitation.

This is the last and final rating. We now know the character not only of the separate components of the design (or layout) but also of the nature and effect of the entire design, package or advertisement.

INDIRECT APPROACH TO MARKET REACTIONS

By Louis Cheskin and L. B. Ward
Harvard Business Review—September, 1948

CHAPTER 19

In This Issue

The Color Research Institute of America has been doing pioneering work in analyzing individuals' reactions to colors and visual patterns. The institute's findings provide the illustrations for an article on "Indirect Approach to Market Reactions" by Louis Cheskin, technical director, Color Research Institute, and L. B. Ward, director of admissions, Harvard Business School. The article makes a pertinent point for management consideration, demonstrating as it does, in a field rich with business applications, the significance of unconscious factors influencing human behavior.

TOP management is often vexed by the apparent inability of sales and marketing personnel to provide definite measurements of such things as the probable effectiveness of a proposed advertisement or the prospects for success of a new product, even when told to "go out and get the answer." It is the purpose of this article to examine one of the major reasons why the matter of market reactions remains less tangible and less directly ascertainable than, say, production costs or engineering specifications, and at the same time to indicate, primarily by way of examples, the kind of approach which may be of help in improving marketing decisions.

Many of the examples used, particularly in the later sections, are drawn from the findings of the Color Research Institute. Although these findings in a sense merely verify some of the factors of human behavior which have been uncovered by other investigators and are by now common knowledge among the experts in marketing research, they have a special interest because they come from an area, rich with possible business applications, that has not previously been explored in any systematic way. The important consideration, regardless of how obvious or how novel the illustrations may be, is to emphasize the fact that many marketing studies are still being made which fail to take into account this available knowledge.

Unconscious Factors of Behavior

Much of the effort put forth in marketing research, in product design, in advertising campaigns, and so on, either is based on the unsound assumption that people consciously consider certain features of a product or is the expression of shrewd "hunches" which happen to be right because they are made by men with wide experience in what will sell. Yet one does not have to be a psychiatrist, psychologist, or specialist in marketing research to know that people buy what they do for all sorts of reasons, many of which they do not consciously consider when they are actually making the purchase.

In its increasing concern with the unconscious determiners of behavior, social science in this country owes a great deal to the psychoanalysts. Although Psychoanalysis still has far to go to meet with unqualified acceptance among scientists in general, many of our modern ideas concerning human behavior are the result of observations stimulated by the psychoanalytic approach.

In any case, there is today fairly general agreement among social scientists that many of our day-by-day actions are determined by factors of which we are not consciously aware. It is, of course, obvious to all of us that we forget most of the details of our daily experiences. What is not so obvious and is often overlooked is that sometimes "forgotten" experiences leave traces which continue to exert tremendous power over behavior. In spite of the common acceptance of the importance of psychological factors, many current attempts to apply the methods of social science to the problems of business and industry still fail to take into account the unconscious habits, purposes, needs, and motives that determine behavior.

One could give innumerable illustrations of ways in which people are unconsciously influenced in their buying. Here is a typical one, from a recent study of the effect of wrapper design upon soap sales in a grocery store. The same bar of soap was placed on the shelves in two different types of wrappers. The soap in one wrapper outsold the soap in the other wrapper nearly two to one. Now it is self-evident that the average housewife does not consciously go to the grocery store to buy package designs; she goes to buy ham, vegetables, soap, canned fruit, and so on. Only rarely does she consciously consider the container in which these items are sold. That those buying the soap in this study were not consciously considering the wrapper in their choice of the soap was shown by their reactions when it was suggested to them that they were buying the soap because of the wrapper. If the women's facial expressions did not mean they thought the observer was crazy, they certainly showed that at the very least they did not value his opinion of their buying practices. Nevertheless there is no question but that the wrapper or package determined which bar of soap was preferred, for it was the only differentiating factor.

Inadequacy of Direct Approach

Probably the most obvious and frequently used procedure in marketing research is to ask individuals what they buy, what advertisements they have seen or heard, why they buy what they do, what types of products they like best, and so on. This is a direct approach, and certainly it often yields information of value. When the questions asked have to do with what a person has actually done recently (e.g., "What brand of coffee did you buy last?"), the answers may be fairly accurate.

Even with such questions, however, people are sometimes unwilling to give the right information, and the answers to specific inquiries may therefore be completely wrong. This point needs little explanation; most well-informed readers are already aware of it. Also, there have been various techniques worked out to compensate for the errors thus introduced. We can be content here with an illustration or two to show the kind of thing that can happen.

A number of people were interviewed in one of the large cities and were asked various questions. To the question, "Do you borrow money from a personal loan company?" all of those interviewed answered "No." Yet all of those interviewed were listed in the records of a local loan company as having recently borrowed money. Another example has to do with the magazines people claim to have read. The answers of a large number of people to the question, "What magazines do you read?" if taken at face value, would lead one to believe that the Atlantic Monthly had six times its actual circulation, while the pulp magazines, printed by the millions, had almost negligible appeal. The desire not to appear "lowbrow" clearly influenced the answers given to this question.

When a person is asked to recall in detail what he

has seen or heard recently—whether, for example, he
has seen a particular advertisement or not—there is
much evidence to show that the answer is even more
likely to be misleading. This point is illustrated by the
following experiment: A number of proof sheets of advertisements for pharmaceutical and medical products
were shown to a group of doctors. Each was asked,
"Have you or have you not seen this advertisement before?" One of the advertisements shown had never been
published, so that it was impossible for the doctors to
have seen it. Yet 12 per cent to 14 per cent of the doctors who took part in the study reported they had seen
the advertisement before. A few weeks later the same
doctors were reinterviewed, and another set of advertisements was shown to them which included the un-
published one used previously. Although this time all
had seen the advertisement since it was shown to them
in the course of the preceding interview, again only
12 per cent to 14 per cent reported having seen it.
Clearly, the answer that the advertisement was or was
not seen had little or nothing to do with whether it had
in fact been seen.

Although the results just cited do not reveal what
effect the advertisement in question had on the many
doctors who saw it but did not remember it, we would
be wrong to draw the conclusion that it had no effect
on them. An indirect type of approach might have
revealed that the doctors were influenced by the advertisement even though they could not recall having seen
it. When a direct question shows individuals do not

recall an experience, an indirect approach often shows that under certain conditions some aspect at least of that experience can be recalled. This is illustrated by what happened in the following experiment:

Forty persons were told to walk through a room and carefully observe its contents. Upon leaving the room each person was asked to write down a list of all of the items seen in the room. One of the articles on one of the tables in the room was a pair of scissors. Only three of the forty people in the experiment recalled having seen the scissors when they listed what they had seen. At this point the scissors were removed from the room, the rest of the items being left as before. Each person was sent back into the room with instructions to cut some simple patterns out of some colored paper that was there. It was evident that scissors were needed to do the job. Of the forty persons, twenty-four now said that they were sure that they had seen a pair of scissors in the room. Yet only three of these had been able to list the scissors as one of the items seen in the room. Evidently the situation of needing the scissors to do something recalled to their minds that they had seen scissors in the room when they were there before.

If there are difficulties in the way of finding out what people have done, and in finding out what has been the effect of what they have seen or heard, it is even more difficult to predict what people will do in the future. One can sometimes tell what one will do in certain situations, but it is difficult to tell what one will do in many other situations. More often than not people just do

213

not know what they will do. They can only tell what they think they will do. Here also an indirect approach will be very revealing and will often show up some of the factors which influence people's behavior.

There is another source of difficulty in much current market research. A common type of study is to ask a number of persons which of several product designs they like best or which of several packages would be preferred for a particular product. Or again, several advertisements may be tried out to discover which attracts the most attention, which is best remembered, and so on. The difficulty with studies of this sort is that out of such studies one learns only which one is the best of the group of advertisements, package designs, or product designs being tested. Little information is obtained as to how good the best really is or how it could be made even better.

What is needed here is knowledge as complete as possible of all of the factors which determine action at the point of sale. While it may never be possible to know all these factors, careful and systematic investigation to determine the nature of the most important ones, through the approach of studying human behavior rather than asking direct questions, will in the long run make for great improvement in marketing procedures. Only then will it be possible properly to plan and evaluate a proposed advertisement, product design, or sales program.

INDIRECT APPROACH TO MARKET REACTIONS

Factors Determining Purchases

What are the factors which determine the buying preferences of the general population or of large segments of the general population? Some of these have to do with the abstract qualities of the article bought: color, brightness, visual pattern, three-dimensional shape and form, feel or texture, odor, and so forth. Others, such as brand name, have to do with common meanings, interpretations, and attitudes which are aroused by some selected feature of the article in question.

Abstract Qualities

One example of an attempt to study systematically some of the abstract factors influencing behavior in situations of special interest to business is found in the work of the Color Research Institute. As its name would suggest, the institute began its studies in the field of color, attempting to analyze the part that color plays in the daily lives of most people. The direct approach was tried first, individuals being asked which of various standard colors they preferred in general. Because of lack of agreement as to the meaning of common color terms, it was, of course, necessary to show these people a sample, usually in the form of a swatch. In this way various colors, hues, tints, and shades were presented with the purpose of finding out which were

liked best. Early in these studies, however, it was observed that the colors people reported they liked best
were not the colors they chose in what they bought or
the colors they kept around or near them. These observations led to an attempt to determine color preferences indirectly. In the indirect studies, the individual
color preferences were derived from the choice of colors
in prizes and rewards offered for participation in what
were ostensibly studies made for some other purpose.

It soon became clear that it would not be necessary
to obtain preference ratings for every different hue,
shade, tint, or color that could be differentiated. It was
found that colors normally affect people according to
certain laws, so that with a knowledge of an individual's
preference with respect to certain particular colors it
becomes possible to predict the degree of liking for
other colors, shades, tints, and so on. For instance, it
was found that certain hues are given progressively
higher preference ratings and others progressively lower
ratings if they are diluted with increasing amounts of
white or neutralized with increasing amounts of gray.
In this connection, it was found that the six main hues
of the visible spectrum form convenient points of ref-
erence for determining color preference. People tend
to adopt either a favorable or unfavorable reaction to
each of these hues. Reactions to other color values
(tints, tones, and shades) and other hues depend on
their closeness to these standards in terms of hue,
tonal value, brightness, and so on. A person may like
the bright blue very well, the light blue a little, and the

lightest blue the least, reacting favorably, however, to all of these. If such a person also does not like green, then hues a little more greenish than the original blue will be chosen less often in proportion to their degree of closeness to the disliked green.

What determines the color preferences of a person? Naturally, there is no complete answer to a question of this sort. At the same time, studies of differences between color preferences of different groups of people have yielded much interesting information. Thus, some hues consistently rate higher with men than with women and vice versa, men seeming to prefer warm orange-red and the sharper tones in general while women apparently favor magenta red, green-blue or turquoise, and the pastel tones. Interestingly enough, men and women are more likely to agree in their preferences when neutral color values having a large component of gray are involved.

The studies using the indirect approach to color preference also revealed that, in addition to the more general or basic color preferences, there are some striking geographical and national or community differences. For instance, it was found that a certain orange-red, although it has a comparatively low rating with all groups of people studied, has a relatively much higher rating with Italians and Mexicans than it does with those of Scandinavian or Northern European backgrounds. Color preference was also found to be related to type of community background. A grass-green color has, for example, a low preference rating among people from rural communities; while with people from a steel mill district it has a very high preference rating.

Although much additional evidence is needed, there are some observations to support the hypothesis that geographical and other factors related to the region where the individual has lived have more to do with degree of liking for "pure' hues (e.g., red as against blue) and so on, while type of community and economic factors within a given community have more influence upon preferences relating to colors differing in value (i.e., tints, tones, and shades of a given hue). All of these conclusions, if substantiated through additional studies, would have some interesting implications with respect to how color preferences are developed. At present any attempt to explain why one group prefers certain colors, while another group prefers others, would be pure speculation, and the explanation would depend entirely upon one's concept of the nature of personality and how individuals develop habits, attitudes, likes and dislikes, and so on.

In this connection it should perhaps be pointed out that in all of these studies where consistent group preferences were obtained, there were also many individuals who showed unusual or extreme reactions with respect to particular colors and individuals whose color preferences were entirely different from the group's. The psychoanalysts have reported some significant observations along this line, claiming to have shown that certain strong color phobias or extreme dislikes could be traced to traumatic experiences in early childhood.

Certain individuals who reported that they disliked a bright red, for example, were found by psychoanalytic technique to have had one or more unpleasant experiences in which this color was somehow involved.

From the studies of colors, it was evident that color alone did not suffice to explain more than a very small part of a person's preference for particular objects, advertisements, and so forth. The shape and visual pattern seen by the individual certainly are important. Again the direct approach, in which the individual is asked which design he prefers, which is the most beautiful of several objects, and so on, yields misleading information. Two examples will illustrate this:

(1) A study was made to find out which of two package designs was preferred. One was very ornate and in five colors, and the other was very simple and in but two colors. The individuals who took part in the study were shown the two designs which were the subject of the study, together with four others included for comparison purposes. They were then asked, "Which of these six package designs do you like best for this product?" The ornate design won by a wide margin.

Then the participants were asked to choose one of several names to be given to the product. Those selecting the name finally given the product were to receive some of the product for prizes. As if incidentally, they were asked to designate in advance in which of the six types of package they wanted their prizes, if they won them, to be sent. Here it was the product name which was the focus of the judgment of the individual, whereas the package was thought of only in terms of which particular package was wanted, not which was the "best" package design. In this part of the study the simple design was far ahead of the ornate, being chosen more than three times as often.

(2) A similar study was made with kerchiefs, popularly known as babushkas. The women taking part in the study were asked which of six kerchiefs was the most beautiful. Nearly all of them chose No. 6. Then a product-naming contest was conducted, with the same women taking part, and they were offered a kerchief as a prize. Of the women who had reported that No. 6 was the most beautiful, only 10 per cent wanted No. 6 as the prize. It was obvious during the study that many of these women picked their prize consciously and deliberately, considering how they would use the kerchief and how it would go with their clothes and complexion.

When people are asked to give their opinion about how good a pattern is or how well they like a color, their attention is focused on the design and the color, and they take on the role of art critics. But in real buying situations people do not ordinarily consider such things as designs or judge them with the same standards. Furthermore, as these studies showed, merely having a favorable attitude toward a design or color is no guarantee that the favorable attitude will find expression in action.

One of the things revealed by these studies was the obviously wide differences among groups of people with respect to their reactions to visual patterns and shapes, despite the fact, again, that many tend consciously to associate intricacy and great detail with "good" art. Among various shapes and patterns, such as ovals, rectangles, triangles, and scrolls, the individual differences in preference that show up are so great that useful generalizations can be made only tentatively. However, some general tendencies were found, such as the fact that a simple oval shape is generally preferred over a rectangle. There is likewise some evidence of a sex difference in preferences of visual patterns, with men preferring angular designs and women curved lines. All in all, the infinite variety of possible visual patterns makes it unlikely that more than the simplest of patterns can be compared as to general preference rating. Furthermore, it is probable that the visual pattern is also one of the main sources of meaning—a most important factor, to be discussed below.

Another aspect of visual experience is that of visibility or what might be called the quality of "strikingness." Obviously, this depends not only upon the object or portion of an object or advertisement in which one is interested but also upon the background in which it appears. Here the degree of contrast between the portion at which attention is directed and the rest of what is in the visual field is one of the important factors. The brightness of what is seen can easily be measured with an optical instrument. Further study may show that the differential between the brightness of the object or advertisement to be studied and that of its surroundings may be useful in estimating visibility. Many other factors, however, would have to be included to get a workable estimate. One of these other factors would be readability of any words that might be a part of the visual pattern. Similarly, the ease of identification of any objects depicted on the wrapper or advertisement, or of any markings on the object, would be an important feature.

In other studies it has been found that there are differences between colors, shapes, odors, patterns, and sounds in terms of how well they tend to be remembered. Certain hues, such as peach, apparently have a high preference rating but are not well recalled. In contrast, yellow, which usually has a low preference rating, tends to be much better recalled. Among visual patterns, the simpler ones tend to be better recalled, even though there does not seem to be a consistent relationship between preference rating and likelihood of recall.

Meanings and Motivations

After one has obtained the common preference ratings with respect to colors, shapes, patterns, sounds, odors, and so on, there still remain certain general reactions related to "meaning" and object use which have been found to modify these preferences in a radical way. In fact it is only by minimizing meaning and considering general use rather than specific use that preferences with respect to these abstract qualities can be determined. Thus, a certain magenta red is one of the highest colors in general preference rating, yet it is given a very low rating as soon as it is related to use in the kitchen. On the other hand, orange-red, with a low preference rating stands much higher when rated in terms of use in the kitchen on walls, kitchen utensils, curtains, and so on. Again, colors of the peach-pink range receive a much higher preference rating than usual when associated with cosmetics and a very much lower rating when associated with hardware, while the reverse is true for colors of the blue family. Certain greens, while given high preference for many situations, have low ratings with respect to food products. A different green has a high preference rating with respect to jewelry and a low rating with respect to cosmetics.

All of these observations illustrate the strong effect of meaning or use. A convenient designation for this effect is the term symbolism used by the psychoanalysts. There is no question but that all types of symbolism have a profound influence upon preferences expressed for colors, shapes, visual patterns, sounds, odors, and so on. All of our reactions to the abstract qualities of immediate experience are clearly influenced by this factor.

There are still many other factors which either consciously or unconsciously influence people's behavior that are of great interest to business. It is rather obvious to everyone that most individuals do not like to appear in an unfavorable light in the eyes of others. This desire to appear well before others is much more important in some situations than it is in others. The psychoanalysts also have a good term for this factor—ego-involvement. Whenever in the buying situation the individual feels that what he buys will favorably influence other people's opinions of him, the psychoanalysts would say that his ego is involved. Put in everyday terms, we all like, consciously or unconsciously, to do the things that maintain our self-respect. Whether or not these things actually do make others think better of us is really not the important thing. The important thing is that we behave as if we believe they do.

Women's fashions certainly bear witness to the importance of this factor. There must be thousands of women who do not personally like the "new look." Yet many of them, though they make a show of protesting, would rather be found dead than appear on the street in a skirt styled around 1940 or 1941. As for men, they will not take off their ties, even when uncomfortable. They do not today wear brightly colored clothes the way they did some generations past or the way men still do in certain other parts of the world. We seek to conform. We seek to fit into the group in which we belong. We tend to feel self-conscious and insecure unless our clothes meet the current styles.

In many buying situations there are conflicting factors present even in individuals. Those selling women's clothes often encounter situations like the following:

In a particular shop a young lady told the saleswoman that one of the dresses fitted her perfectly, just as if it had been designed for her figure. The dress was avail-

able in four colors—coral, fuchsia, turquoise, and chartreuse. The young lady mentioned right away that she
did not like the coral. She found it hard to make up her
mind about the fuchsia, a color which she had been told
many times flattered her complexion, or the chartreuse,
which was featured in the fashion magazine she had
read, or the turquoise, which she thought was such a
beautiful color. The psychology of the situation might
be roughly summarized like this: in the case of the
coral and turquoise models she was reacting primarily
in terms of whether or not she liked the color in general, whereas in the case of the fuchsia and chartreuse
she was conscious of the fact that one improved her
appearance and that people would consider her stylish
if she wore the other.

Assuming the young lady in the previous example
could buy only one dress, which would she choose?
That obviously depends on what kind of person she
was as well as on her feelings of the moment. If she
were an especially self-confident and independent sort
of person who did not care much about people's opinions on styles, she would probably have chosen the
turquoise blue, which she liked as a color. If she felt
especially self-conscious about her complexion and
wished to improve her appearance in that respect, she
would probably have chosen the fuchsia. If she were
concerned about social recognition and thought especially of styles, she would probably have chosen the
chartreuse even if she had despised the color.

Although the evidence is so far only suggestive, interviews with women immediately after they have purchased garments show that where there is a conflict between natural color preference and the desire either to appear in style or to choose a color that improves personal appearance, only about 20 per cent choose the color of their natural preferences, with the style and personal appearance motivations each accounting for 40 per cent of the choices. This shows the dominant part played by factors other than abstract qualities in the type of situation being considered here.

There is some evidence, on the other hand, that although at the time of buying the desire to be in style or to purchase what we believe will enhance our standing with others is dominant, at the point of use natural preferences are sometimes stronger. Thus in cases where women have bought the same dress in two colors, one a color much in style and the other a color they especially like, they tend to wear the one they like more often than the one whose color is in style. In one case a woman had bought two coats—one because "they're wearing blue this season," the other because she liked beige. In four weeks she wore the blue coat three times and the beige coat twenty-one times.

Needless to say, the factors other than color influencing the purchase of fashion goods are considerably more extensive and complex. Such oversimplification as that used in the above example is in line with the primary objective of this article—to show the kind of progress that purposeful research can make in a definite area, which is of course only a part of a much larger picture.

INDIRECT APPROACH TO MARKET REACTIONS

Studies such as these have a number of implications for marketing and merchandising. Not only do we need to know about the market's natural preferences in terms of color, shape, and so on, but we need also to consider the other unconscious reasons for the choices that people make. Thus, in advertising, if we desire to utilize the natural preferences of various buying groups on such things as color, the appeal should be in terms of situations with the appropriate meanings and motivations. Indeed, where competing products for sale are of about the same quality, as is the case, for example, with cigarettes and with so many other articles, motivation for buying a particular brand must be aroused in terms of some factor of a more complex sort, such as the desire to be in style, to follow custom, to gain prestige, and so on.

The influence of these factors and the extent to which the advertising is successful in arousing the desired motivation can be determined only by use of indirect methods of approach to the segments of the market to be studied. Asking the individual why he bought what he did, or what he thought of an advertisement, is not likely to reveal the true reasons or the true effects. If businessmen in general paid more attention to these indirect methods of determining what will sell and if systematic studies were carried on to show what are the common types of motivation leading to action, much time and money would be saved.

RIGHT COLOR COMBINATIONS
MAY LEAD TO SUCCESS IN
BUSINESS, ROMANCE

By Lucia Perrigo; Spot News, King Features Syndicate—
May 30, 1947

CHAPTER 20

WAS our face red, to coin a cliché, when we wandered into the office of the Color Research Institute the other day and discovered how blind we were to color.

George D. Gaw and Louis Cheskin, the two gentlemen who run this amazing Chicago menage, came up with the crumbs of comfort that although comparatively few persons are color blind, the masses on the whole are blind to a knowledge of color and how hues affect their lives.

Businesses have prospered or failed because of color and that goes for marriages, too, they point out. You may feel in the pink or downright blue and do not kid yourself that gray days do not have a lot to do with it.

You cannot escape color, but you can make it work for you. Cheskin and Gaw have proved it—and very profitably.

* * *

RIGHT COLOR COMBINATIONS

Cheskin, sitting in his peach and blue-green office, expounded:

"Actually black is the worst of all colors—extremely negative psychologically, but by contrast it makes a woman look more beautiful.

"Many a girl thinks her most flattering dress color is red, yellow or green. But for most women, the most becoming dress is black. Compliment her on a pink dress and you virtually say, 'What a beautiful dress.' Ah, but compliment her on a black gown and you say, 'What a beautiful figure!' "

Because black is a negation, it makes adjacent colors more vibrant and more beautiful and is definitely in romantic cahoots with a woman who has a naturally clear complexion or well-applied makeup.

It makes the skin look pinker, richer and clearer and outlines the contours of the figure.

However, if you have a drab complexion, the two implore you to wear a touch of white near your face. If dark-complexioned, stick to gay accessories like a creditor to a debtor.

At the other extreme, white has a favorable symbolic meaning and therefore has some psychological value since it is associated with cleanliness and purity. It is neither sedative nor stimulating, but is often flattering since it reflects light more than any other color and thus illuminates the skin.

Now, the cagey customer will wear gray, a neutral, which will provide a favorable background for him and any accessory he might choose for that day. Gray plays no tricks on you, but shows you off as you truly are.

If blondes would be preferred by gentlemen, Cheskin pointed out, they would do well not to highlight white in their wardrobe since they do not need its illuminating effect and white does not give enough contrast to their skin. It definitely does not display the figure to best advantage as any three-year-old can see by walking south of a white-clad dowager walking north.

*   *   *

Because women count allure as a very handy asset, the clothes-conscious blonde who wears blue knows the value of color. The blue, being complementary to yellow, makes her blond hair look even more so; while the brunette should wear light warm colors of the yellow family, such as beige, light brown, cocoa.

The titian-haired woman who yearns to be a redhead can get aqua to help her turn the trick. The redhead should run from red or her hair will look as rusty as a rain barrel on May 1.

The brownette need use the least skill in selecting her colors as most any will co-operate.

Besides analyzing colors for packaging and advertising art, the institute put red blood back into the business of a large chain of restaurants whose patronage had dwindled to pathetic proportion.

The owner had thought white tile on the walls gave a clean atmosphere conducive to appetite. Not until he added color did the patronage perk up. This, Cheskin believes, was due to the fact that most people associate white with hospitals and thus find it depressing.

*   *   *

"White can postpone a patient's recovery," he explained, "and different ailments require different color schemes. I think one of my favorite stories concerns a cafeteria in an Eastern plant where during a vacation period the walls were changed from peach to blue.

"The workers began to complain that the room was cold and some even wore sweaters to lunch. Engineers got nowhere by pointing out that the rheostat showed the temperature was unchanged. Then when the walls were changed back to peach the complaints stopped."

This color sensation has often been found to act upon people who are completely unaware of the presence of color, the visual sensation producing physical reaction. People will feel cold in a blue room and hot in a red one, the former being a sedative color soothing to highly nervous people, while the latter is stimulating. Color preference tests, for example, have demonstrated that reds, blues and violets (half of the color circle) are much more popular than oranges, yellows and greens. Most popular color with men is blue; with women, red, which ought to give you an inkling into the desire of the male animal!

Proof positive that color plays an important part in the enjoyment of food was demonstrated recently at a dinner party given by an illuminating engineer. At the dinner table when the guests took their seats were the finest of dishes, definitely a gourmet's binge.

Suddenly, the lighting was switched from white to colored bulbs, the steaks turned gray, the celery pink, the salad violet, the peas black as caviar, the milk red, the eggs blue and the coffee a jaundiced java. Most of the guests immediately lost their appetites. In short, the dinner was a failure, but the experiment a success.

* * *

Color Research, in working with many meat markets, has discovered that the best color for decorating them is blue-green which serves to make the meat appear redder and more palatable.

Milk does not taste as well in colored glasses, and people will turn up their noses at orange juice that has been colored like tomato juice, though the taste is not altered—and that goes for Californians, too!

Children, like primitive peoples, are attracted to pure hues only, and while a baby pink may thrill mama, the two-to-six-year-old likes it red hot, his favorite color. Infants cannot identify orange or purple. Orange is associated with red or yellow while if you tell a tot the color is purple, not blue, he is likely to identify blue as purple.

As for color blindness, these authorities tell you that it is only in pairs of complementary colors, except in cases of partial disintegration of a color nerve.

Blindness to red and green is much more common than blindness to blue and yellow. Although three to four men out of 100 are color-blind, only one out of 300 women are thus afflicted.

If all this leaves you in the dark, the institute will be glad to bring light upon the subject, because, as it points out, it is as cheap to use color correctly and intelligently as it is to use the wrong color for you psychologically and, in some cases, professionally. Inspect the spectrum with intelligence, and, if you are a businessman, you can make the colors of the rainbow lead you to that pot o'gold.

INDEX

INDEX

INDEX

H

Hardware, 121, 184, 187
Harvard Business Review, 20, 49, 86, 207
Hawley and Hoops, 75
Horney, Karen, 34

I

Image, brand identifying, 77, 87, 95, 103, 108, 110, 153
Image effect, 133
Image preference, 39, 40
Image retention, 120
Image symbolism, 118, 119
Image tests, 39, 40
Imagery, accumulated data, 51, 52
Imagery, preference ratings, 51, 52
Imagery, realistic, 157
Impact, 50
Imperial margarine, 74
Indirect approach, 212, 214
Indirect methods, 227
Indirect preference tests, 36, 37, 63, 64, 69
Indirect preference tests, sampling, 63
Indirect techniques, 87
Industrial interiors, 108
Industrial packaging, 124
Institute of Motivational Research, 18
Interviewing technique, 57
Interviews, 30, 211, 212
Intricacy, 186, 221

J

Jacobsson, E. G., 169
Jewelry, 154
Jung, Carl, 34

K

Kitchen colors, 175
Koffka, Kurt, 35
Kohler, Wolfgang, 35

L

Laminates, 74
Lever Brothers Company, 72, 74, 105, 106, 162, 164, 169
Libby's Deep-Brown Beans, 187
Libido, 128
Lippincott and Margulies, 73, 169
Lux Toilet Soap, 71, 72, 105-107

M

Margarine, 60, 74, 107, 108, 128, 150, 151, 162, 164
Marlboro, cigarettes, 72, 87, 89, 99, 104, 105
Mars Confections, 75
Meanings, 222
Motivation Research, definition, 84, 85

Involuntary reactions, 46, 47, 51, 52, 78

INDEX

240

INDEX